· PAUL E. BILLHEIMER ·

DON'T WASTE

your

SORROWS

D1537251

BETHANY HOUSE PUBLISHERS

Minneapolis, Minnesota

Published by Bethany House Publishers
11400 Hampshire Avenue South
Bloomington, Minnesota 55438

Bethany House Publishers is a division of
Baker Publishing Group, Grand Rapids, Michigan.

Printed in the United States of America

Library of Congress Cataloging-in-Publication Data

Billheimer, Paul E.
    Don't waste your sorrows : finding God's purpose in the midst of pain / Paul E. Billheimer.
        p.   cm.
    Summary: "No Pain, no gain. In this now recognized classic, Billheimer gives hope to those in pain—it's all part of the training. Count the painful 'why God?' moments in life as character building for eternity"—Provided by publisher.
        ISBN 0-7642-0158-1 (pbk.)
        1. Suffering—Religious aspects—Christianity. 2. Agape. I. Title.
        BT732.7.B46   2006
        231'.8—dc22   2005033246

PAUL E. BILLHEIMER and his wife began a tent ministry in Anderson, Indiana, in 1936 that grew to include a Bible institute, a Christian high school, a Christian day school, and a Christian television station. In later years they worked with Trinity Broadcasting Network. They were married for sixty-three years and raised three children. Billheimer passed away in 1984.

A Word *from* the Author

In this book I affirm that the universe, including our planet, was created to provide a suitable habitation for the human race. Humankind was created in the image and likeness of God to provide an eternal bride for the Son. After the fall, and the promise of redemption, the Messiah was sent to earth for one purpose: to give birth to His church, the bride of Christ.

God's purpose from all eternity has been to gather a people for Christ's bride, to train them and prepare them for their exalted position of co-rulership with the Son over His vast and eternal kingdom.

In my book *Destined for the Throne* I explained that prayer is more than a method for getting things done (God is self-sufficient); rather it is on-the-job training for the bride in overcoming the forces hostile to God and His purposes. Overcoming is a prerequisite to ruling with Him.

In this volume, suffering is considered another aspect of our training. Suffering produces in us character and a proper disposition—a compassionate spirit. Being born again launches us into a kind of apprenticeship in training for rulership. True agape love (God's perfect love)¹ is developed in the school of tribulation, trial, or suffering.

God makes us pure through the sacrifice of His Son; trials and testings make us mature.

Contents

FOREWORD

I was pleased indeed with the volume *Destined for the Throne*, but I am thrilled with *Don't Waste Your Sorrows*. The insights and vantage points gained in the former volume have enabled the author to see deeply and clearly into one of the darkest and most mysterious valleys of human existence—the problem of suffering and sorrow. He shows how God uses it as a precious means of developing character here on earth and thereby making possible for the child of God as he enters the heavenly realm "a far more exceeding and eternal weight of glory."

Most materials written on the subject of sorrow leave the reader with questions. In this volume we find an answer that is clear and biblical, based on the character and being of God. The concept of God and man suffering together, eternal values thereby accruing—impossible to achieve in any other way—helps to transmute sorrow and suffering into closer communion with the Lord.

The presentation of agape love in this book transcends most treatments of the love motif by a unified coverage of its achievement here and its reward as rank in the kingdom of God. *Don't Waste Your Sorrows* shows pain and suffering not to be an oversight or accident, but part of the eternal love-plan of God for perfecting His bride on earth for her place in the eternal kingdom of God.

In centuries past millions of Christians have gone through suffering and death to receive a martyr's crown. There is no reason to doubt that millions of Christians now living may meet similar persecution and even martyrdom. *Don't Waste Your Sorrows* will prepare readers for unexpected testing and help them to rejoice as they suffer for Christ.

—DR. B. H. PEARSON
 Author, missionary,
 President emeritus of World Gospel Crusades
 Upland, California

INTRODUCTION

Today there is a strong emphasis in certain religious circles that insists the ideal spiritual life is one of unbroken joy, peace, and material prosperity. The impression is given that to be saved and filled with the Spirit opens a charmed life that is trouble-free, where problems are instantly solved and miracles are common.

Some go so far as to say that unless miracles are the norm there is something wrong between the believer and God. To some the Spirit-filled life is one long roller coaster ride, a picnic, a lark. No one should ever be sick, and if he is he should seek immediate healing. If he needs money, all that is needed is to ask God and the heavens will open. If one does not live in affluence he is missing something spiritually. Even if this is an exaggeration, it illustrates the point.

There is a measure of truth in this theology in that few of us live up to our spiritual privilege. God would like to manifest His generosity and miracle-working power far more than is normally seen. But the question is whether this philosophy is in proper spiritual perspective and balance or whether it represents only one side of the coin.

The other side of the coin is represented by the concept of the Christian life as a spiritual warfare that demands courage, sacrifice, and self-discipline. This theology stresses the unavoidable weariness, toil, and pain that is sometimes encountered; the bitterness of conflict, the occasional desperate days and dark, distressful nights. This side is also represented by the record of the noble army of martyrs whose blood has proved to be the very seed of the church. It is further seen in literature that has exalted and glorified heroic courage, valor, self-denial, and the high cost of true discipleship.

Reginald Heber wrote the words to the hymn that speaks of a Christianity few can identify with today:

> *The Son of God goes forth to war,*
> *A kingly crown to gain;*
> *His blood-red banner streams afar:*
> *Who follows in His train?*
> *Who best can drink His cup of woe,*
> *Triumphant over pain?*
> *Who patient bears the cross below,*
> *He follows in His train.*

Amy Carmichael directed Dohnavur Fellowship from her invalid's bed for many years. She wrote the words to "The Soldier's Prayer":

> *From prayer that asks that I may be*
> *Sheltered from winds that beat on Thee,*
> *From fearing when I should aspire,*

From faltering when I should climb higher,
From silken self, O Captain, free
Thy soldier who would follow Thee.

From subtle love of softening things,
From easy choices, weakenings,
(Not thus are spirits fortified,
Not this way went the Crucified).
From all that dims Thy Calvary,
O Lamb of God, deliver me.

Give me the love that leads the way,
The faith that nothing can dismay,
The hope no disappointments tire,
The passion that will burn like fire.
Let me not sink to be a clod:
Make me Thy fuel, Flame of God.[1]

The soldier theme was immortalized by C. T. Studd in the statement "If Jesus Christ be God and died for me, then no sacrifice can be too great for me to make for Him."

Norman Grubb, director of the Christian Literature Crusade for many years, pointed out that the Holy Spirit in the life of the believer will drive him to a life of suffering sacrifice just as He did in the life of Jesus.

In her book *What About Us Who Are Not Healed?* Carmen Benson voices the doubts, fears, and perplexities of the multitudes who, without apparent reason, seek healing without success.

One might ask, "Is the life of unbroken peace, joy, prosperity, health, and happiness spiritually superior? Does it bring the most glory to God? And are those who fall short of this ideal second-class citizens of the kingdom?"

Some rejoice in the measure of faith that produces success, prosperity, and healing. We recognize that miracles of healing and other great answers to prayer exalt the Lord and triumph over our adversary. Demonstrations of supernatural signs and wonders are scriptural and confound unbelief, stimulate faith, and draw souls to the Lord.

But how can the apparent failures in the Christian life be explained? Some are healed, but multitudes are not. A few have miraculous answers to prayer for healing and prosperity, but most do not. Are those in the larger category to give up in self-pity and defeat? Must the one who is not healed or delivered suffer with a sense of spiritual inferiority? Or is it possible for the great majority who remain financially limited or physically afflicted to make as great a contribution to the kingdom and bring as much joy to the heart of God and win as great an eternal reward as those who are favored with supernatural deliverance here and now?

Could it be that this question may be answered in the affirmative?

WHAT PRICE GLORY?

*For our light and momentary troubles are achieving
for us an eternal glory that far outweighs them all.
So we fix our eyes not on what is seen, but on
what is unseen. For what is seen is temporary,
but what is unseen is eternal.*

2 CORINTHIANS 4:17–18

In order to understand this passage, it is necessary to define the term *troubles*. (The King James Version has *affliction*.) It is probable that Paul was thinking primarily about the persecutions, opposition, deprivations, and hardships that he and the early Christians faced in their devotion to and promotion of the gospel message.

Those troubles Paul suffered personally are partially detailed in 2 Corinthians 11:23–33. Among them were many experiences that produced physical suffering and possibly permanent injury. Many doubt that Paul's "thorn in the flesh" (2 Corinthians 12:7) was a physical illness, but that interpretation is not out of the question.

The original Greek word translated "trouble" or "affliction," simply means "pressure." According to *Webster's New World Dictionary*, affliction is anything causing pain or distress. It implies any sorrow, suffering, or heartache imposed by illness, loss, misfortune.

Some believers conclude that God may use other types of

trouble to discipline an erring saint or one who needs further child-training, but not physical illness, because Jesus took upon himself our infirmities and bore our pains on the cross (Isaiah 53:4–5).

Because of Jesus' sacrifice, they believe that it is *never* necessary to accept illness as disciplinary. Since the price has been paid for deliverance, they insist that a believer should be able to exercise faith for immediate healing without waiting to learn the new lesson God may be seeking to teach through the affliction.

This seems to be contrary to Paul's understanding in 1 Corinthians 11:28–32: "A man ought to examine himself before he eats of the bread and drinks of the cup. For anyone who eats and drinks without recognizing the body of the Lord eats and drinks judgment on himself. That is why many among you are weak and sick, and a number of you have fallen asleep. But if we judged ourselves, we would not come under judgment. When we are judged by the Lord, we are being disciplined so that we will not be condemned with the world."

Here it seems that God is using physical affliction to discipline believers. If so, then it is impossible to rule out sickness as a means the Lord may use to focus the attention of a believer upon some area of his life that needs correction. Alexander Maclaren has said that every affliction comes with a message from the heart of God. Watchman Nee said that we never learn anything new about God except by adversity. Again, David said, "Before I was afflicted [evidently physically] I went astray, but now I obey your word. It was good for me to be afflicted so that I might learn your decrees" (Psalm 119:67, 71). Finally, Job is an example of God's disciplinary use of physical affliction.

Thus, it seems that although Jesus did take our infirmities and carry our pains, God does use physical affliction to chasten His children. If so, then we may not rule out sickness and disease as included in the "light and momentary troubles" that Paul says may achieve "for us an eternal glory that far outweighs them all."

If we accept this interpretation of affliction, then Paul is saying that "trouble" from any cause, including bodily pain or suffering (even when no healing follows), may work for our good. If this is possible, then believers who are suffering in the flesh and have failed to obtain healing should cease their lamentation, mourning, self-pity, and depression, and instead seek the way by which their suffering and sorrow may be for their eternal benefit. This book is an attempt to help the suffering find this way.

Life's Most Serious Problem

Except for sin, sorrow is life's most serious problem. According to *The New Testament and Wycliffe Bible Commentary*, the verb that is translated "achieving," in the original also means "to create." This being true, the apostle is saying that our momentary troubles, properly accepted, are actually creating or producing for us an eternal glory that exceeds the pain of the affliction. Therefore, it should be cherished and not *wasted* by resistance and rebellion.

Paul further amplifies this glorious truth of our theme passage (2 Corinthians 4:17–18) in Romans 8:18, "I consider that our present sufferings are not worth comparing with the glory that will be revealed in us." And in Romans 5:3–5, "Not only so, but we also rejoice in our sufferings, because we know that suffering produces perseverance; perseverance, character; and character, hope. And hope does not disappoint us, because God has poured out his love [agape love] into our hearts by the Holy Spirit, whom he has given us."

To many, this is pure wishful thinking, and to accept it is little more than "whistling in the dark." This book, based on solid logic and scriptural reality, is an attempt to show that this concept is more than just a morale builder.

Sorrow or suffering poses what has probably been through the ages the most troubling problem for believers. Suffering is not only the last thing to be considered useful but also something to be avoided, evaded, shunned. But as we have seen, according to the Word of God, suffering is not an accident, but a gift to be valued, for when properly received it works to enhance our eternal rank and honor.

— *Suffering Is Universal*

In a fallen world, suffering of some kind is universal. There is no permanent release or escape from it, either by rank, holy living, health, or wealth. "Man is born to trouble as surely as sparks fly upward" (Job 5:7). "In this world you will have trouble" (John 16:33). "But of course you know that such troubles are a part of God's plan for us Christians. Even while we were still with you we warned you ahead of time that suffering would soon come— and it did" (1 Thessalonians 3:3–4 TLB). Trouble, therefore, comes to us all, whether saint or sinner.

— *The Sinner Has Sorrow*

We are not surprised that the sinner has sorrow. "There will be trouble and distress for every human being who does evil" (Romans 2:9). We understand that trouble and sorrow always follow sin. This is an immutable law. Although the sinner may fail to comprehend this, sin and sorrow are synonymous. "The wages of sin is death" (Romans 6:23).

— *Why Does a Saint Suffer?*

But why should the righteous suffer? Why isn't every believer healed, and immediately at that? Why isn't he, as the songwriter says, "carried to the skies on flowery beds of ease"? Why must he "fight to win the prize and sail through bloody seas"? It is difficult for most people to understand why sorrow comes to a faithful Christian. It is one of the mysteries of the ages. However, regardless of the mystery involved, we know that God is love and that, according to 2 Corinthians 4:17–18, He permits suffering to the Christian only to achieve (create) for him an "eternal glory." No one ever becomes a saint without suffering, because suffering, properly accepted, is the pathway to glory.

THE CHIEF SUFFERER *in the* UNIVERSE

The Suffering of the Godhead

Human beings are not the only ones who suffer in the universe. There is a tendency to suppose that the God who decreed the penalty for sin did so arbitrarily and is himself unaffected by His decree. The supposition is that He is immune, entirely insulated from the suffering of the penalties He has imposed upon sinners. The idea is widely accepted that He hurls His thunderbolts of wrath that bring sorrow and heartbreak to others from a so-called ivory tower of isolation. Although He created a world in which sorrow reigns (after the fall), the accusation is that He himself is untouched by its ravages and pangs.

But I submit to you that this is not so. You may be surprised by this statement: The infinitely happy God is the supreme sufferer in the universe. From all eternity, before He spoke the world into existence, before angels or archangels, cherubim or seraphim, before the first member of the human race was created in the image and likeness of God, God anticipated the fall and ordained the plan for human redemption. And He knew this could not be accomplished without suffering to the Godhead. Nor could one worship as God one who is immune (sheltered) from suffering, because agape love, which is the essence of godlike character, would then be lacking. It is the *slain Lamb*, the *One* who as a man suffered, who is acclaimed by the innumerable glorified throng in the book of Revelation as worthy to receive power and wealth and wisdom and strength and honor and glory and praise! (5:12).

God's Purpose—A Generic Family

God's original purpose in creation was to obtain a generic (descriptive of all members of a species) family of His very own, not created only but also generated or begotten anew. "Long ago, even before he made the world, God chose us to be his very own [generically] through what Christ would do for us; he decided then to make us holy in his eyes, without a single fault—we who stand before him covered with his love. His unchanging plan has always been to adopt' us into his own family by sending Jesus Christ to die for us" (Ephesians 1:4–5 TLB). "For from the very beginning God decided that those who came to him—and all along he knew who would—should become like his Son, so that his Son would be the First, with many brothers" (Romans 8:29 TLB).

— The Purpose of the Generic Family

But that was not all. The purpose of this generic family was to provide an eternal companion for the Son, called "the bride, the wife of the Lamb" (Revelation 21:9). In God's plan, this eternal companion is to be trained and elevated to the throne of the universe as co-regent with her Bridegroom following the wedding supper of the Lamb (Revelation 3:21; 19:7, 9). But God knew that His bride could not be obtained without infinite suffering to the Godhead. He also knew that the bride could not be prepared for her queenly role without her suffering. If God was to realize His purpose in creation, to obtain an eternal companion for His Son, He himself had to suffer. It was unavoidable. And if the bride was to be qualified to rule with Him, she also had to suffer. This illuminates the passage in 2 Timothy 2:12, "If we suffer, we shall also reign with him" (KJV). *Therefore, suffering is inherent in God's universe.* And if this is true, suffering must perform an infinitely valuable service. It must be of supreme importance.

Suffering Is Inherent in God's Economy

Because God wanted His bride-elect to love him voluntarily, He was compelled to give her an option. This option involved the possibility of sin (the fall). Sin requires redemption. Redemption required the atonement. The atonement required suffering. *Therefore, from all eternity, suffering is inherent in God's economy.*

The Cost of a Voluntary Love

When God conceived the plan of creation and redemption, He knew about the fall of mankind in advance and accepted the necessary fact of infinite suffering, of His experiencing the total consequences of the cumulative sin of the world with its resultant sickness, sorrow, suffering, and pain. He knew He could not make a full atonement for sin without actually experiencing in His own being the suffering that eternal justice demanded for the transgression of the universal moral law. He therefore planned in advance to come to earth as a man; it is of the God-man, Jesus, that we are told: "During the days of Jesus' life on earth, he offered up prayers and petitions with loud cries and tears to the one who could save him from death, and he was heard because of his reverent submission. Although he was a son, he learned obedience from what he suffered" (Hebrews 5:7–8). He also knew in advance that his suffering had to be of the same quality and intensity of that which accompanied the sin of the sinner.

⁓ Not a Bookkeeping Process

That the Godhead voluntarily accepted the certainty of suffering the full penalty and consequences of the cumulative sin of the race in order to obtain His eternal companion is therefore a logical and necessary corollary of the atonement. If Jesus did not actually experience in His own person the full penalty of the sin of the human race, the atonement would be merely a bookkeeping process that could in no way satisfy eternal justice. And eternal justice could not survive if it merely ignored the sin of our race. Under universal jurisprudence, the penalty of every sin of all of humankind had to be paid by someone to balance the scales of the law's demands. This is why Christ, the Lamb of Revelation 13:8, is said to have been "slain from the creation of the world." *Suffering is inherent in a universe that is moral.*

A MORAL UNIVERSE

Three Kinds of Love

What is meant by a universe that is moral? It is one in which the law of love is supreme, because love is the fulfilling of the law. It fulfills every obligation to every intelligence in the universe, whether to God, man, or angelic beings. The most fundamental characteristic of an order that is moral, therefore, is *agape* love. There are three Greek words that are translated "love": *eros*—the love between the sexes; *philos*—the love of friendship and family; and *agape*—the love that characterizes God himself. You will remember that *agape* love is the love that loves because of its own inherent nature, not because of the excellence or worth of its object. According to the Bible dictionary, it is a spontaneous, automatic love. To illustrate: The sun shines alike upon fragrant flower gardens and reeking dung heaps because it is its nature to shine. It cannot help it. In the same way, God's love embraces good and evil personalities alike, pouring out sunshine and rain equally upon the righteous and the unrighteous (Matthew 5:45). "God *is* love" (1 John 4:8). He is personified love. He consists of love, which is His essence. First Corinthians 13 is a divinely inspired description of *agape* love. *Agape* love is not primarily an emotion, but aggressive, benevolent, sacrificial, outgoing goodwill. It is the soul of ethics.

The Omnipotence of Love

Because God is love, love must be the one all-powerful principle in the universe. Otherwise, God could not be God. The syllogism would be stated thus: God is all-powerful. God is love. Therefore love is all-powerful. *Since this is true, love is the all-enduring, everlasting, supreme principle of the universe.* Satan challenged this principle and lost. According to Revelation 12, there was war in heaven, and Satan and his angels were cast out. However, he still believes that brute force is more powerful than love. He is the power behind the beast of Revelation and, according to modern satanism, still expects to dethrone God.

According to *The Satanic Bible*, the crucifix symbolizes "pallid incompetence hanging on a tree." In *The Satanic Rituals*, Satan is called "the ineffable Prince of Darkness who rules the earth." He is further seen as seizing the initiative from Christ, who is called "the lasting foulness of Bethlehem," "the cursed Nazarene," "impotent king," "fugitive and mute God," "vile and abhorred pretender to the majesty of Satan."

Satan is described as "Lucifer who rules the earth" and who will send the "Christian minions staggering to their doom." He is also depicted as the "Lord of Light"—with Christ's angels, cherubim, and seraphim "cowering and trembling with fear" and "prostrating themselves before him," while he "sends the gates of heaven crashing down."

— The Ultimate Triumph of Love

The book of Revelation tells a different story. It describes a conflict between a wild beast, representing brute force, and a slain Lamb. The conflict ends with the beast forever banished and the Lamb on the throne of the universe with the bride at His side as co-regent. *Love has won!* When "the heavens shall pass away with a great noise, and the elements shall melt with fervent heat, and

the earth also and the works that are therein shall be burned
up . . . look for new heavens and the new earth, wherein
dwelleth righteousness" (2 Peter 3:10, 13 KJV); when they
replace a ruined and purged universe, only that which has come
to terms with love will remain. *This love is even now, this present
moment, the supreme law of the universe and will survive and outlast all its
rivals.*

The Purpose of Life on Earth

Because this is true, learning agape love as personified in Christ
is the supreme purpose of life on earth. This is the meaning of
all that God permits to come to one of His children. God's primary occupation in this age is not regulating the universe by the
mighty power of His command, but it is teaching the members
of His bride-elect the lessons of agape love in preparation for
the throne. He is doing nothing in the realm of redemption that
is not related to this task. Therefore, every single incident,
whether of joy or sorrow, bane or blessing, pain or pleasure,
without exception is being utilized by God for the purpose of
procuring the members of His bride and maturing them in
agape love. Thus, the supreme purpose of life on earth is not
pleasure, fame, wealth, or any other form of worldly success, but
learning agape love. In the ultimate social order of the universe
(the kingdom of God) rank will be determined not by talent,
magnetic personality, intellectual acumen, earthly success and
affluence, but by one characteristic and one alone—agape love.

"Jesus . . . said, 'You know that the rulers of the Gentiles lord
it over them, and their high officials exercise authority over
them. Not so with you. Instead, whoever wants to become great
among you, must be your servant, and whoever wants to be first
must be your slave—just as the Son of Man did not come to be

served, but to serve, and to give his life as a ransom for many'" (Matthew 20:25–28).

Love Suffers

There is no love without self-giving. There is no self-giving without pain. Therefore, there is no love without suffering. Suffering is an essential ingredient of agape love and therefore of a moral universe. Even God cannot love without cost. If you think that the infinitely happy God cannot suffer, think what it must have cost Him to give His Son to die as a sinner and a sin offering on the cross. Think what it must have cost Him to turn His face away from His innocent Son and forsake Him "who had no sin to be sin for us, so that in him we might become the righteousness of God" (2 Corinthians 5:21). Think also what it must have cost Him to see the Son of His love descend into hell and be delivered to the torments of Satan and the demons for their pleasure (Ephesians 4:9; Acts 2:27). And think what it must have cost Him to pour out upon Him—on the cross and in hell—the full fury of His own wrath against sin because of the guilt of the cumulative sin of all mankind (Hebrews 2:9).¹

— *Love Suffers Voluntarily*

The apostle Paul said, "Love suffers long and is kind" (1 Corinthians 13:4 NKJV). The NIV says, "Love is patient, love is kind. It does not envy, it does not boast, it is not proud." This kind of behavior involves a choice. God is love, but there is no love without voluntary suffering. Love that does not accept suffering voluntarily is a misnomer, for the essence of love is decentralization, that is, repudiation of self on behalf of another. Therefore, in the universal absolute sense, there is no character without suffering. Suffering love is the cornerstone of the universe, because without it there is no denying of the self and therefore no expression of agape love. One who has never voluntarily suffered is a self-centered individual. Only great sufferers are truly benevolent.

LEGAL DELIVERANCE

Legal Deliverance
Through Christ's Sufferings

———

Because Christ could not make a full atonement for sin without absorbing its full consequences in His own person and being, no human being can ever suffer a pain, sorrow, heartache, or disappointment that Christ has not already experienced in His own person.

Isaiah 53, the great atonement chapter, affirms: "Surely he took up our infirmities and carried *our* sorrows . . . he was pierced for our transgressions, he was crushed for our iniquities; the punishment that brought us peace was upon him, and by his wounds we are healed" (vv. 4–5). In the context of Christ's healing ministry, Matthew translates this: "'He took up *our* infirmities and carried *our* diseases'" (Matthew 8:17, emphasis added).

Verse 6 of Isaiah 53 states: "We all, like sheep, have gone astray, each of us has turned to his own way; and the LORD has laid on him the iniquity of us all." Therefore, the total penalty— all the sorrow, suffering, pain, poverty, and disease—the full consequences of the cumulative sins of all of Adam's race, was laid upon Him. What is the meaning of all of this for the suffering believer? It means that every born-again believer is legally delivered from the full penalty, all the bitter fruits of sin and the fall. This penalty cannot legally be collected the second time.

The prophet said, "By his wounds we are healed" (v. 5). If this is so, then every believer is legally delivered from all sickness, disease, pain, sorrow, poverty, and limitations of every kind.

— What Is Legal Deliverance?

Through Adam's fall, all of his progeny became bona fide slaves of Satan. He possessed the power of death over them. But because Jesus was born of the Virgin Mary without a human father, and so was not a mere son of Adam, Satan had no legal right to touch Him. Previously, Satan had slain his millions with impunity. When he *illegally* slew Jesus upon the cross, for the first time in history Satan legally became a murderer. This brought upon him the sentence of death. A person under the sentence of death has no legal standing, rights, or claims. He is legally destroyed. This is what the writer to the Hebrews meant when he said that through death Jesus destroyed (rendered powerless) "him who holds the power of death—that is, the devil" (2:14). Therefore, since Calvary, Satan has no *legal authority* over any believer. The believer's faith has translated him out of the dominion of darkness (Satan's authority) and into the kingdom of the Son God loves (Colossians 1:13).

Although Satan is legally destroyed, and has no lawful authority over the believer, God uses him as an opponent to train the bride-elect in overcoming and in learning agape love. Thus, when God allows Satan to afflict one of His children, it is not because Satan has any legal right to do so, but rather in order to train God's child in overcoming and in learning deeper dimensions of agape love. Because Satan lost all of his claims at Calvary, every child of God is legitimately delivered from all of his affliction and oppression. All that God permits to remain is only for our training purposes. The apostle Paul understood this when he said that our light affliction is working for us (2 Corinthians 4:17–18 NKJV).

When one is delivered from affliction by faith here and now, that one has triumphed. When the symptoms persist and he has learned a new dimension of agape love, he has also triumphed because he has increased his eternal rank.

The Universal Scope of the Atonement

In the Word, therefore, there is a perfect theology of health and prosperity. From Genesis to Revelation run the glad tidings that the atonement covers the entire scope of human need. The more than thirty-two thousand promises assure us that all we need for body, soul, and spirit for both time and eternity is provided in the atonement. Nothing could be more sweeping than Philippians 4:19: "My God will meet all your needs according to his glorious riches in Christ Jesus." Also 3 John 2: "Dear friend, I pray that you may enjoy good health and that all may go well with you, even as your soul is getting along well." These promises are amplified and supported by thousands of others promoting health and well-being to God's obedient people.

— *A Clear Theology of Health and Prosperity*

From the beginning God promised both temporal and spiritual blessings to Israel as long as she was obedient: "If you listen carefully to the voice of the LORD your God and do what is right in his eyes, if you pay attention to his commands and keep all his decrees, I will not bring on you any of the diseases I brought on the Egyptians, for I am the LORD, who heals you" (Exodus 15:26). Also read Leviticus 26:3–10 and Deuteronomy 28.

The theme is continued in the record of the healing miracles of Jesus in the Gospels, in those of the apostles in Acts, and reaches a distinct confirmation in James 5:14–15: "Is any one of you sick? He should call the elders of the church to pray over him and anoint him with oil in the name of the Lord. And the prayer offered in faith will make the sick person well; the Lord will raise him up. If he has sinned, he will be forgiven."

— *The Early Church—God's Prototype*

It appears there is as distinct a theology in the Word for health and prosperity as there is for salvation. Many believe that the first century church is God's prototype for the entire age, that we are still in the dispensation of the Holy Spirit, and that if God had His way, all the gifts of the Spirit would be present and manifest in the church today in a similar proportion as in the early church. Many are convinced from the Word that health and prosperity are God's first and best choice for His obedient children. All other things being equal, He would prefer our health to our illness.

How could it be otherwise? The Lord taught His disciples to pray: "'Your will be done on earth as it is in heaven'" (Matthew 6:10). We are sure there is no sickness or poverty in that fair land. Since these are the result of sin, they cannot be God's preferential will, because sin and all of its effects are against the will of God. Hallelujah! The entire universe is moving toward a social order called the kingdom of God, where none of these can exist (Revelation 21:4-5; 22:2-5). Therefore, they cannot be God's choice at any time for any part of His dominion. All of God's universe-wide activity is directed toward the total elimination of sin and all of its consequences from all spheres of His redeemed creation.

Since all of these things are true, why should any obedient child of God suffer? Not because God wills it as such, or because He has not made provision for its eradication, but because the ultimate goal of the universe is a social order where agape love is supreme.

THE MYSTERY *of* SUFFERING

Love Is the Norm of the Universe

God is calling and preparing an eternal companion, called the bride, who is to sit with His Son on His throne as His co-regent in the ages to come (Revelation 3:21). In order to qualify for this exalted position, the members of the bride *must* be as nearly like the Son as it is possible for the finite to be like the infinite. If they are to qualify for their lofty duties, they *must* share the character of God himself, which is agape love. This is the norm of the universe, the ideal toward which God is working for the eternal social order. But as we have seen, that quality of character cannot be developed in fallen humanity without suffering (see chapter 3).

— Glory and Suffering

This explains Paul's inspired revelation: "If we suffer, we shall also reign with him" (2 Timothy 2:12 KJV). According to Romans 5:3–5, suffering issues in character (agape love), and character is a prerequisite to rulership. Because there is no character development without suffering, suffering is a necessary preparation for a place of ruling.

Massive Damage of the Fall

God pronounced the unfallen Adam "very good," but the fall brought massive damage to Adam and all of his progeny. It left the race self-centered. Selfishness is the very essence of all sin and misery and results in self-destruction. It is the core of hostility, which is the core of hell, or the hallmark and essence of it. Self-centeredness is the antithesis of holiness, or agape love, which is the hallmark and essence of heaven.

— *The Necessity of Decentralization*

In bringing an individual into the likeness of His Son, God must decentralize him. This process begins in the crisis of justification and the new birth and continues in the experience of sanctification or the filling with the Holy Spirit. Of necessity, it does not end there. These are only beginning experiences, similar to a vestibule, which is a good place to enter, but not a place to stay. The work of sanctification, by which selfishness is dealt with, is both instantaneous and progressive. It is both a crisis and a process, which continues throughout life in a healthy Christian. "And I am sure that God who began the good work within you will keep right on helping you grow in his grace until his task within you is finally finished on that day when Jesus Christ returns" (Philippians 1:6 TLB).

The Work of Tribulation

If God's net purpose in saving an individual were to get him to heaven, He would probably have taken him to glory immediately. But God wants to prepare us for rulership in an infinite universe that demands character. Progress in sanctification, in the development of godlike character and agape love, is impossible without tribulation and chastisement. "Not only so, but we also rejoice in our sufferings, because we know that suffering produces perseverance; perseverance, character; and character, hope. And hope does not disappoint us, because God has

poured out his love into our hearts by the Holy Spirit, whom he
has given us" (Romans 5:3–5).

"'My son, don't be angry when the Lord punishes you. Don't
be discouraged when he has to show you where you are wrong.
For when he punishes you, it proves that he loves you. When
he whips you, it proves that you are really his child.' Let God
train you, for he is doing what any loving father does for his
children. Whoever heard of a son who was never corrected? If
God doesn't punish you when you need it, as other fathers punish their sons, then it means that you aren't really God's son at
all—that you don't really belong in his family. . . . Our earthly
fathers trained us for a few brief years, doing the best for us that
they knew how, but God's correction is always right and for our
best good, that we may share his holiness [character]. Being
punished isn't enjoyable while it is happening—it hurts! But
afterward we can see the result, *a quiet growth in grace and character*"
(Hebrews 12:5–8, 10–11 TLB, emphasis added).

> *I walked a mile with Pleasure*
> *She chattered all the way*
> *But left me none the wiser*
> *For all she had to say.*
>
> *I walked a mile with Sorrow*
> *And ne'er a word said she*
> *But oh! the things I learned from her*
> *When Sorrow walked with me.*
> *—Robert Browning Hamilton*

— Chastisement and Child Training
It is clear from the foregoing and other similar passages of
Scripture that sorrow, suffering, tribulation, and pain that come

to the believer are not primarily for punishment but for child training. They are not purposeless. Earthly parents may make mistakes in their chastisement—and often do. But God does not. He is preparing the believer for rulership in a universe so vast that it appears infinite. It seems that God cannot fully decentralize fallen man, even though born again, sanctified, and filled with the Holy Spirit, without suffering. Watchman Nee says that we never learn anything new about God except through adversity. Some consider this an exaggeration, but it does seem that few seek a deeper walk with God except under duress.

THE EXAMPLE OF ISRAEL

The history of Israel illustrates this point. In prosperity, she forsook pure Jehovah worship for licentious idolatry. Only by chastisement was she constrained to repent and return to Jehovah. For centuries, while God was seeking to obtain a pure remnant through whom He could bring the Messiah, it was the same routine: prosperity, backsliding, and apostasy; chastisement, repentance, and return to God ad infinitum (Judges 2:11–19; 1 Samuel 12:9–10; 2 Chronicles 15:4, 33:12; Isaiah 26:16).

THE EXAMPLE OF THE PSALMIST

The experience of the psalmist is illustrative: "Before I was afflicted I went astray, but now I obey your word. It was good for me to be afflicted so that I might learn your decrees" (Psalm 119:67, 71). Who of us have not known people with Christian background and training who have wandered far from God and have been brought back to Him through heart attack, cancer, tragic accident, or some other severe addiction?

THE EXAMPLE OF CHRIST

One of the most amazing commentaries on the purposefulness of suffering in the economy of God is set forth in

Hebrews 2:10: "In bringing many sons to glory, it was fitting that God, for whom and through whom everything exists, should make the author of their salvation perfect through suffering." And Hebrews 5:8 says, "Although he was a son, he learned obedience from what he suffered."

In Christ's case, according to Alexander Maclaren, "His perfecting was not the perfecting of moral character, but the completion of His equipment for His work as leader and originator of our salvation. Before He suffers, He has the pity of God. After He suffers, He has the compassion of a man."[1] *The New Testament and Wycliffe Bible Commentary* says: "By suffering his *human* experience was made complete. . . . Because he suffered he is now fully qualified to serve as captain (*archegos*, leader) of man's salvation."[2] If the "many sons" whom Christ was to bring to glory and rulership had to be prepared and perfected for that glory by suffering, their Captain must lead the way by having His human experience perfected in the same way. The fact that Christ's human experience had to be perfected by suffering proves that no suffering is purposeless, but that it is endemic in God's economy.

The Importance of Brokenness

Christ's suffering only matured and perfected His human experience. It purged nothing from His moral nature, even as a man, because He was unfallen. No stain of sin ever marred His humanity. But this is not the case with fallen man. There is no way that Christlike character can be formed in man without suffering, because he cannot be decentralized any other way. If he will not suffer, if he determines to evade it, if he refuses to allow the life of nature and of self to go to the cross, to that extent he will remain hard, self-centered, unbroken, and therefore, not Christlike. "Whole, unbruised, unbroken men are of little use to

God," said J. R. Miller. By his self-will one may escape a certain quality of pain, that which accompanies self-immolation, but in so doing he becomes the victim of a far greater pain, that of self-worship. He cannot escape both. Someone has said, "There are things that even God cannot do for us unless He allows us to suffer."

— *The Pain of Moral Choice*
Oswald Chambers says that "God does not make us holy in the sense of character; He makes us holy in the sense of innocence, and we have to turn that innocence into holy character by a series of moral choices. These choices are continually in antagonism to the entrenchments of our natural life."[3]

There can be no spiritual progress, therefore, except through the progressive death of the self-life. Maclaren has said that every step on the pathway of spiritual progress will be marked by the bloody footprints of wounded self-love. All along the course of spiritual advancement one will have to set up altars upon which even the legitimate self-life will have to be sacrificed.

To make the moral choices that develop godlike character always causes pain, because even after one has been sanctified and filled with the Holy Spirit, one is still a fallen being. Some people feel that after these experiences of grace, nothing remains in their spiritual life with which God has a controversy. But the work of sanctification is both instantaneous and progressive. It will continue until our glorification.

Sheridan Baker, a writer in the early holiness movement, said: "But there is much to be done for the believer in the way of chastening, and melting, and mellowing, after this state [the Spirit's baptism] is reached, and consequently, it is not a finality in the process of redemption. . . . The purified believer will not be long in discovering rudeness in his manners which he will deplore and escape, roughness in his speech and tone of voice which he will deprecate and abandon, and other dregs of the old disease which will cling to him, though the disease itself has been removed and from which he will escape 'little by little' as beautifully symbolized by the conquest of Canaan."[4]

The Spiritually Static State Is a Vice

One of the greatest vices of the church is a static state of grace. The fruit of a grapevine is always on the new growth. This is the reason for pruning the vine. Without new growth there is little or no fruit. This is why Jesus said, "He cuts off every branch in me that bears no fruit, while every branch that does bear fruit he prunes so that it will be even more fruitful" (John 15:2). If the branch had sensibility, pruning would be painful. But without suffering there would be neither growth nor fruitfulness.

Annie Johnson Flint has beautifully expressed this truth:

It is the branch that bears the fruit,
That feels the knife
To prune it for a larger growth,
A fuller life.

Though every budding twig be lopped,
And every grace
Of swaying tendril, springing leaf,
Be lost a space,

O thou whose life of joy seems reft,
Of beauty shorn;

Whose aspirations lie in dust,
All bruised and torn,

Rejoice, tho' each desire, each dream,
Each hope of thine
Shall fall and fade; it is the hand
Of Love Divine

That holds the knife, that cuts and breaks
With tenderest touch,
That thou, whose life has borne some fruit
May'st now bear much.[5]

Self-Pity Is a Waste

How meaningful are the words of Jesus in John 15:1, "My Father is the gardener"—not Satan, but *My Father*. Not understanding God's benevolent purpose when sorrow and suffering come—whether as the result of conflict over moral choices, of pain and physical illness, or of disappointing circumstances—it is easy to fall into a spirit of resentment and self-pity, which produces frustration and depression. When this occurs, one is defeated in his spiritual life and character deteriorates. *He has wasted his sorrow.* What God permitted in order to wean him from self-love and self-worship, and therefore for his spiritual growth, has resulted in loss.

— *Comfort From Pain*

How often one is tempted to question, even mourn the years of disability, invalidism, and pain suffered by saints such as Madame Guyon, Fanny Crosby, Amy Carmichael, George

Matheson, and others, out of whose suffering God distilled
sweet comfort, healing, and strength for millions of fainting pil-
grims. God's frequent transmutation of sorrow into blessing for
others is beautifully expressed in these lines by an unknown
author:

> *Out of the presses of pain*
> *Cometh the soul's best wine;*
> *And the eyes that have shed no rain*
> *Can shed but little shine.*

This, of course, illustrates only the temporal situation, not
the eternal glory, which is perceived only as one fastens his
vision upon the "things that are not seen."

— *Character From Affliction*

Suffering, from whatever source, of whatever nature, and of
whatever intensity, plus triumphant acceptance, equals character
(Romans 5:3–4). Character (agape love) is the coin, the legal
tender of heaven. Therefore, "our light affliction, which is but
for a moment, is working for us a far more exceeding and eternal weight of glory" (2 Corinthians 4:17 NKJV), that is, an
exceedingly higher rank. Affliction, triumphantly accepted here,
means rank there, because this is the way God builds selfless
character and develops agape love. Suffering, triumphantly
accepted, slays the self-life, delivers one from self-centeredness,
and frees one to love.

Those who have thus suffered will form the elite, the aris-
tocracy, the ruling nobility of the future. They will constitute
the princes of the ethereal realm.

Blessed Be Sorrow

In order to grow in character it is necessary to understand that nothing that God permits to come to His child, whether "good" or "ill," is accidental or without design. Everything is intended to drive him out of himself and into God. "All of life is intended to be a pathway to God" (Maclaren). All is for the purpose of character training. *There are no exceptions.* God neither slumbers nor sleeps (Psalm 121:4). Because God is the all-seeing One, Satan cannot "slip up on His blind side." He is never taken by surprise. Only this faith will enable one to understand the statement: "Blessed be sorrow."

— *Blessed Be Frustration and Pain*

God cannot train us without mystifying us, even baffling us. Evidently God has objectives for us that cannot be achieved apart from frustration and bewildering pain. Faith cannot be perfected except by apparent denial. This was the way Job's faith was perfected, so that he said, "Though he slay me, yet will I trust Him" (Job 13:15 NKJV). This is the kind of faith that does not depend upon tangible fulfillment. It cannot be developed without our being utterly frustrated. God cannot develop this quality of faith in us without His appearing to deny himself. Indeed, He may sometimes need to appear to be false, as in the case of Job. Or He may sometimes seem to be unfaithful, as in the case of Abraham's offering up Isaac when God's promise and command appeared to be in diametric opposition. In Abraham's case, faith was led to the very edge of the precipice. And this meant suffering, probably the most unendurable of all. Until one has weathered this kind of testing and trial of faith, he cannot identify with the unknown author of the following lines:

I will not doubt, though all my ships at sea
Come drifting home with broken masts and sails;

I will believe the hand which never fails,
From seeming evil worketh good for me.
And though I weep because those sails are tattered,
Still will I cry, while my best hopes lie shattered:
"I trust in Thee."

I will not doubt, though sorrows fall like rain,
And troubles swarm like bees about a hive.
I will believe the heights for which I strive
Are only reached by anguish and by pain;
And though I groan and writhe beneath my crosses,
I yet shall see through my severest losses
The greater gain.

The Mystery of Healing That Does Not Come

This is the kind of suffering that plagues many who seek healing. They realize there is a perfect theology of healing. They know that the atonement is full and complete. They fully believe that Jesus himself has borne their sicknesses and carried their pains. They are convinced that they are legally delivered from all oppression of the devil. Yet the faith that brings actual deliverance from the symptoms seems unobtainable. Sometimes this goes on for years, and even unto death. Some are healed, but many are not. Some are given achieving faith and are miraculously restored, while others are not.

A FAITH GREATER
THAN ACHIEVING FAITH

The Greatest Eternal Profit

Until recently, during all the years of my ministry, I have been under the solid impression that supernatural healing and deliverance here and now *always* brings more glory to God and more eternal profit to the individual than continued suffering. For those who are healed, this is probably true. A sovereign God knows what He is doing. But for those who are not healed, may it not be otherwise? There is something to be said for this viewpoint. If the goal of the universe is character—that is, a disposition of agape love—and if character cannot be created without tribulation, then may not the discipline of tribulation produce in both time and eternity as desirable a result, if not a better one? *The answer lies in our reaction to the discipline.* Resentment and rebellion only "waste one's sorrows," whereas humble acceptance and brokenness allows the creation of an "eternal glory."

Great Sainthood
Often Means Great Suffering

It is not unusual that the greatest saints—those who have made the greatest contribution to the kingdom on earth—are those who have suffered the most. The world never would have heard of Madame Guyon, and the church never would have been enriched by the fragrance of her life, and perhaps eternity would have been poorer, if it had not been for her victory over tribulation. If ever a person could have wasted her sorrow, it was she. By the depth of her triumphant submission, her sufferings were transmuted into character, which has left an indelible mark upon the spiritual life of succeeding generations and probably enriched heaven. Among those influenced by her life and witness was the sainted Fenelon. Would it have been better for the kingdom, would it have brought more glory to Christ, would her eternal rank have been more exalted, if Madame Guyon had been healed of smallpox and spared the crushing humiliation and sorrows that followed in its wake?

It seems possible, even probable, that Madame Guyon's eternal worth and service, her contribution to the eternal kingdom, was enhanced more by the way she was enabled to triumph in adversity of every kind, especially ill health, than it would have been had she been miraculously healed. It seems possible that the completeness of her submission and triumphant faith in the wisdom and goodness of her Lord brought more joy and satisfaction to His heart than would have a miracle-working faith for healing and deliverance. The faith that can truly say, "Though He slay me, yet will I trust Him" may be more precious in God's sight than faith that moves mountains, because it may arise out of a more self-sacrificial love. The words of the great apostle support this:

"If I speak in the tongues of men and of angels, but have not love, I am only a resounding gong or a clanging cymbal. If I have the gift of prophecy and can fathom all mysteries and all knowledge, and if I have a faith that can move mountains, but have not love, I am nothing" (1 Corinthians 13:1–2). It was Madame Guyon's unutterable love for her Lord that enabled her to triumph over suffering, pain, and unspeakable misfortune, including the loss by death of her children and loved ones.[1]

Could it be that the many others who seek and fail to find healing have as great or greater opportunity to glorify God by accepting suffering triumphantly, as she did, and developing the character of agape love, which is the legal tender of heaven?

Heroes of Faith of Hebrews 11

Hebrews 11 may illuminate this question. From verse 32 through the first part of verse 35 is the record of the heroes of faith who were gloriously, miraculously, and supernaturally delivered. There is nothing like it outside the annals of sacred history. Among other spectacular deliverances recorded, such as those of Daniel from the lion's den and the three Hebrew children from the fiery furnace, mention is made of supernatural healing when "weakness was turned to strength" (v. 34), and others were raised from the dead (v. 35).

But another order of heroes of faith is listed beginning in the middle of verse 35: "Others were tortured and refused to be released, so that they might gain a better resurrection. Some faced jeers and flogging, while still others were chained and put in prison. They were stoned; they were sawn in two; they were put to death by sword. They went about in sheepskins and goatskins, destitute, persecuted and mistreated" (vv. 35–37). According to verse 39, "These were all commended for their faith, yet none of them received what had been promised."

— The Heroism of Faithful Endurance

Does anyone believe that those who were delivered were more highly commended for their faith than those who were not? Does anyone doubt that as high or higher a degree of love was demonstrated by those who suffered but endured without deliverance, as by those who enjoyed the miraculous? Because the law of love is supreme in the eternal social order, is it not possible that the army of saints who proved their sacrificial love by "climbing the steep ascent to heaven through peril, toil, and pain," wandering about "in sheepskins and goatskins, living in dens and caves of the earth"—is it not possible that they may be of equal rank with those who were miraculously delivered? Because agape love is the legal tender of heaven, when the rewards are meted out in that day, it may be that those who joyfully "drank their cup of woe" by enduring destitution, affliction, and torment will be of comparable or higher rank than those who escaped by supernatural intervention.

What Does It Mean to Suffer *With* Christ?

We usually think of the afflictions that Paul says are "working for us an eternal weight of glory" as probably in the category of severe persecution or martyrdom. It has been said that in the last twenty-five years more people have suffered severe persecution and martyrdom for Christ than in any other similar period of history. Some of us may yet be called upon to prove our faith and love by accepting a martyr's crown. But at this point, at least in the United States, the adversity to which most believers are subject is not the danger of martyrdom or other types of persecution. Today, the American believer's afflictions are mostly physical, financial, or in the area of personality conflicts. Is this type of suffering included in the "light afflictions" that Paul said are working for us? Is this what he meant when he said if we suffer we shall also reign and if we suffer we may be glorified together?

The answer may be that it is not always the character of the affliction that determines its spiritual value, but rather the length of its continuation and one's reaction to it. Whether the suffering is for and *with* Christ may be determined not so much by its nature and severity as by the quality of one's spirit in which it is faced. For example, to live sweetly with a brute of a man, or a contentious, faithless woman, or an ungrateful, contemptuous, wayward son or daughter, or to live self-sacrificially with a helpless, hopeless invalid for years or for a lifetime, may provide the opportunity to develop martyr strength and a deep dimension of love as truly as severe persecution for Christ's sake.

All affliction is intended to drive us to God. It is intended to work a fuller submission, a more utter devotion, an increasing patience, a greater beauty of spirit, a more selfless love toward both God and man. When it accomplishes this, then it may be classified as suffering *with* Christ and for His sake because it has enabled Him to achieve His end and purpose in us. It may require a lifetime of God's dealing in discipline and chastisement to produce the true martyr spirit. When suffering of any degree is allowed to work in us a deeper dimension of agape love, is it not indeed suffering with Christ?

The Triumph of Submission

Is it possible that affliction, which one is now suffering and from which he has long and earnestly sought relief, enable him to join the noble army of the heroes of faith in Hebrews 11? Can we join that noble band by facing our illness or other self-crucifying situations in submission and triumph? It seems that Madame Guyon did just that. If the spirit in which she faced and triumphed over her afflictions and sorrows brought more glory to Christ than her deliverance would have, is it not possible that others who are not delivered may do likewise by the way they face their difficulties? May not the multitudes who seek and fail to receive healing, by a proper subjective attitude of submission and courage in their afflictions transmute them into "a far more exceeding and eternal weight of glory" as did those in Hebrews 11? The answer is yes, when they demonstrate a like victory over tribulation.

The Heroism of Patient Plodding

It seems to some that a life ended swiftly by an act of martyrdom may be more heroic and a greater testimony of deathless love than a long life of faithfulness in the ordinary trials and tribulations of daily life. But may it not be that God is obtaining a similar quality of selfless devotion and sacrificial love through patient endurance of the routine sorrow, suffering, disappointments, heartaches, and pain that He permits as a part of His loving child training? If so, then those who suffer triumphantly, accepting the things that hurt and mar with submission, thanksgiving, and praise, may be enhancing their eternal rank in a similar way as did the martyrs. By a proper reaction while in the school of suffering, they may be learning and demonstrating a quality of agape love that is preparing them for rulership as truly as though they had suffered martyrdom.

On the other hand, yielding to self-pity, depression, and rebellion is a waste of sorrow. Those who have unsuccessfully sought healing and who submit to resentment, discontent, impatience, and bitterness against God are wasting what God intended for growth in love and thus for enhanced rank in the eternal kingdom.

THE GREAT BUSINESS *of* LIFE—
LEARNING AGAPE LOVE, PART 1

Nominees for Exalted Rank

Maybe God cannot get some of the rare saints He needs for certain exclusive and highly specialized vocations in His eternal kingdom any other way than by permitting them to suffer catastrophic losses, sorrow, and pain. If so, then those who have sought healing in vain while others around them are delivered, need not abandon themselves to self-pity, depression, and hopelessness. God may have nominated them for a more exalted rank in His future kingdom than can be attained without the apprenticeship in suffering that produces a purer and loftier love. Instead of relapsing into discouragement, resentment, and defeat—which is a waste of their sorrows—it is their privilege to take advantage of their suffering and cause it to "work for them." The apostle Paul says that if one accepts it as from the Lord and rejoices in the suffering, it will be transmuted into eternal glory out of all comparison with the momentary troubles (Romans 5:3; 2 Corinthians 4:17). Those who are not healed may not need to accept second-class citizenship after all, but may be nominated for enhanced rank and eternal glory.

Our Times Are in God's Hands— Not Satan's (Psalm 31:15)

There is nothing accidental in the life of an obedient child of God. All born-again believers are in training for rulership. God himself is personally supervising the training of His Son's eternal companion who is to be His governing elite following the marriage supper of the Lamb. "The hands that were pierced do move the wheels of human history and mold the circumstances of individual lives" (Alexander Maclaren).

My times are in Thy hand:
My God, I wish them there;
My life, my friends, my soul I leave
Entirely to Thy care.

My times are in Thy hand:
Why should I doubt or fear?
My Father's hand will never cause
His child a needless tear.
—William F. Lloyd

Necessary Pain

God himself specifically chooses the tools and instruments that He knows are needed to fashion and qualify His bride for the unique sphere of her operation and service in the eternal kingdom. Someone has said that the turning lathe that has the sharpest knives produces the finest work. When God makes a saint, He uses the sharpest knives on His turning lathe as well. He cannot shape one without pain, but He never uses needless pain. All is chosen in relationship to one's eternal vocation. In some overwhelming catastrophe one may be tempted to say, "Lord, anything but this." An unknown writer explains it thus:

No chance hath brought this ill to me;
  'Tis God's own hand, so let it be.
He seeth what I cannot see—
  There is a need-be for each pain,
And He one day will make it plain
  That earthly loss is heavenly gain.
Like a piece of tapestry
  Viewed from the back appears to be
Naught but threads tangled hopelessly;
  But in the front a picture rare
Rewards the worker for his care,
  Proving his skill and patience rare.
Thou art the Workman, I the frame,
  Lord, for the glory of Thy Name,
Perfect Thine image in the same.
        —Based on Psalm 119:167-175

This Thing Is From Me

Laura A. Barter Snow has beautifully amplified this truth in her comments on 1 Kings 12:24, in the tract *This Thing Is From Me*.

My child, I have a message for you today; let Me whisper it in your ear, that it may gild with glory any storm clouds that may arise, and smooth the rough places upon which you may have to tread. It is short, only five words, but let them sink into your inmost soul; use them as a pillow upon which to rest your weary head: *"This thing is from Me."*

Have you ever thought of it, that all that concerns you concerns Me too? For "He that toucheth you toucheth the apple of [mine] eye" (Zechariah 2:8). "You are precious in my sight" (Isaiah 43:4). Therefore, it is My special delight to educate you.

I would have you learn when temptations assail you, and the "enemy comes in like a flood," that this thing is from Me, that your weakness needs My might, and your safety lies in letting Me fight for you.

Are you in difficult circumstances, surrounded by people who do not understand you, who never consult your taste, who put you in the background? This thing is from Me. I am the God of circumstances. Thou camest not to thy place by accident, it is the very place God meant for thee.

Have you not asked to be made humble? See then, I have placed you in the very school where the lesson is taught; your surroundings and companions are only working out My will.

Are you in money difficulties? Is it hard to make both ends meet? This thing is from Me, for I am your purse-bearer and would have you draw from and depend upon Me. My supplies are limitless (Philippians 4:19). I would have you prove My promises. Let it not be said of you, "In this thing you did not believe the Lord your God" (Deuteronomy 1:32).

Are you passing through a night of sorrow? This thing is from Me. I am the "Man of sorrows and acquainted with grief." I have let earthly comforters fail you, that by turning to Me you may obtain everlasting consolation (2 Thessalonians 2:16–17). Have you longed to do some great work for Me and instead been laid aside on a bed of pain and weakness? This thing is from Me. I could not get your attention in your busy days and I want to teach you some of My deepest lessons. "They also serve who only stand and wait." Some of My greatest workers are those shut out from active service that they may learn to wield the weapon of prayer.

This day I place in your hand this pot of holy oil. Make use of it freely, my child. Let every circumstance that arises, every word that pains you, every interruption that would make you impatient, every revelation of your weakness be anointed with it. The sting will go as you learn to see *Me* in all things.

God's Full-Time Occupation

There is no sense to sentiments like these unless God is working in us for eternity. Except for the preparation of her many-mansioned home (John 14:2–3), training the bride for the throne is His sole occupation. No other cosmology makes sense or harmonizes with the Word (Romans 8:28). According to this cosmology all that God has done from all eternity and all that He is doing now throughout His infinite domain is related to the preparation of the bride for her heavenly role.' Preparing the kingdom for her and her for the kingdom is His full-time occupation. All that He does until the marriage supper of the Lamb is concentrated on this.

Everything that is permitted to come to any member of the bride has been thoroughly thought out. "And he has showered down upon us the richness of his grace—for how well he understands us and knows what is best for us at all times" (Ephesians 1:8 TLB). Thus, when sorrow or suffering come, one may know that it is not accidental or uncontrolled. It is meant to be that way and is intended for one's eternal welfare, promotion, and glory.

The High Rank of the Redeemed

It is easy to doubt the cosmology that holds that the ultimate goal of the universe is the church. It is easy to question the surpassing importance to God of *one* of His children. In order for one to understand God's supreme interest in him personally, he must remember that redeemed humanity is the highest order of beings in the universe next to the Trinity. The proof of this is that every born-again person is a generic member of the family of God.[2]

> Through the new birth we become bona fide members of the original cosmic family (Ephesians 3:15), actual generated sons of God (1 John 3:2), "partakers of the divine nature" (2 Peter 1:4), begotten by Him, impregnated with His "genes,"[3] called the "seed" or "sperma" of God (1 John 5:1, 18; 1 Peter 1:3, 23), and bearing His heredity. Thus, through the new birth—and I speak reverently—we become the "next of kin" to the Trinity, a kind of extension of the Godhead. . . . Here is a completely new, unique, and exclusive order of beings that may be called a "new species." *There is nothing like it in all the kingdoms of infinity.*[4]

All other orders of beings in the universe are created only. Redeemed humanity is both created and generated.

The Only Valid Explanation of the Universe

When a born-again person understands who he is and what God's purpose for him is, he can better comprehend why God takes such infinite pains with him. He is God's very own beloved child (1 John 3:2). The Father's mercies are over all of His creation from highest to lowest. His love embraces all, from the tiniest insect that basks in the sunlight for a few brief hours and vanishes forever, to the highest archangel in the blazing glory of the vaulted heavens. But only redeemed humanity are members of God's own household and family (Ephesians 2:19). This is the reason why His care is so minute that the very hairs of our head are numbered. This, and this alone, explains the universe. It is the only cosmology that makes sense. All of the vast physical universe with its countless rolling orbs is not intrinsically important. All derive their value from their relationship to God's plan and purpose for His generic family. Because it is related to a redeemed personality, a single hair of the head of one of His children concerns Him more than the multiplied galactic systems with their blazing suns, moons, and planets as they fill the heavens and ride their orbits in outer space.

— *Not Fantasy*

Whatever God does, anywhere in His infinite universe, is not done merely as a manifestation of His power, or for the sake of the inhabitants of outer space, or for the angelic hosts, but for the sake of His very own generic family, members of His own household. If He creates a new galaxy, it is for their sake. If He originates a new order of angelic beings, it is for them (Hebrews 1:14). When He laid down His life on Calvary, it was not for angels or archangels, cherubim or seraphim, or for any of the other inhabitants of the unseen world, but for human beings made in His own image, who will constitute His bride. "Consider the incredible love that the Father has shown us in allowing us to be called 'children of God'—and that is not just what we are called, *but what we are*. Our heredity on the Godward side is no mere figure of speech" (1 John 3:1 PHILLIPS).

— *A Mind-Boggling Cosmology*

This cosmology boggles the human mind—but unless the words of Scripture are meaningless, it is the only valid explanation of the universe. "'No eye has seen, no ear has heard, no mind has conceived what God has prepared for those who love him'—but God has revealed it to us by his Spirit. The Spirit searches all things, even the deep things of God" (1 Corinthians 2:9–10).

Only the Spirit can make this meaningful. When one realizes, even faintly, who he is; and knows that all that comes to him, whether of well-being or of woe, is merely God's way of preparing him for royalty as the "elite of the elite" in the future social order; and that the more severe the discipline, the higher his eternal rank—then he can, with the apostle Paul, thank God always for all things and glory in the tribulation that is creating for him an eternal glory. Only this faith can save us from wasting our sorrows.

God's Method of Teaching Agape Love

It was this kind of faith that inspired J. R. Miller to write: "Whole, unbruised, unbroken men are of little use to God." They are of little use because they are deficient in agape love. Miller says that agape love has to be *learned*—and that is the great business of life. It is the great business of life because the law of love is the supreme law of eternity. But this love has to be learned within the confines of time and only upon this earth in an environment just like it affords. All the circumstances of this life are arranged for this one purpose: to enable one to learn agape love in order to be qualified to administer the law of love in eternity. Natural affection does not have to be learned, but agape love is learned only by being utterly broken, by suffering without resentment. H. E. H. King has beautifully voiced this faith in the following lines:

Here and here alone,
Is given thee to suffer for God's sake;
In other worlds we shall more perfectly
Serve Him and love Him, praise Him, work for Him,
Grow near and nearer Him with all delight,

But then we shall not any more be called
To suffer, which is our appointment here.
   Canst thou not suffer, then, one hour or two?

If He should call thee from thy cross today,
   Saying, "It is finished—that hard cross of thine,
From which thou prayest for deliverance,"
   Thinkest thou not some passion of regret
Would overcome thee? Thou wouldst say, "So soon?
   Let me go back and suffer yet a while
More patiently—I have not yet praised God."

THE GREAT BUSINESS *of* LIFE—
LEARNING AGAPE LOVE, PART 2

The Lame Take the Prey

It is not generally known that George D. Watson, a leader in
the early holiness movement, suffered a devastating lapse in his
early ministry. Years later, after this disaster had done its work
of purging and purifying in his life, he said that God uses for
His glory those people and things that are most perfectly broken. . . . Those who are broken in wealth, broken in self-will,
broken in their ambitions, broken in their beautiful ideals, broken in worldly reputation, broken in their affections, broken in
health, those who are despised and seem utterly forlorn and
helpless, these are the ones the Holy Spirit is seizing upon and
using for God's glory. "The lame take the prey" (Isaiah 33:23
KJV).

Henry Ward Beecher, who reportedly also suffered a similar
catastrophe in his life, said, "Do not be afraid to suffer. Do not
be afraid to be overthrown. It is by being cast down and not
destroyed; it is by being shaken to pieces, and the pieces torn
to shreds, that men become men of might, and that one a host."

Measure thy life by loss and not by gain,
Not by the wine drunk, but by the wine poured forth.

For love's strength standeth in love's sacrifice,
And he who suffers most has most to give.

—*Elisabeth Elliot*

Time—The Vestibule of Eternity

This is utterly contrary to modern psychology. It makes no sense apart from the apostle Paul's cosmology, which understands that the unseen is the real and that time is only the vestibule of eternity. According to modern psychology, a robust ego is necessary for success in an egocentric world. But in that social order that is the wave of the future, the law of love, of self-forgetfulness, and selflessness, is supreme.

To function in that social order one must be decentralized. This requires brokenness, which, properly accepted, secures utter deliverance from self-regard and is the basis of agape love. Calvary love, the love that took Christ to the cross, is the supreme qualification for rulership in the new order of things to come. That quality of love is learned only in time and in a fallen world, as one yields to be broken. The full-time occupation of the enthroned bride will be to express God's love-nature throughout the universe unto the ages of the ages.

The Broken Violin

The principle, value, and use of brokenness even in this present order of things is illustrated by J. R. Miller in one of his books.[1] He tells of a world-famous violinist who hired the services of the most renowned violin maker of his day. At the time appointed, the violinist returned to take delivery of the instrument he had authorized. Taking it in his hands, he skillfully drew the bow across the strings. Great disappointment swept over his face. The quality of tone did not satisfy his artistic ear. Raising the violin over his head, he smashed it to pieces on the table, paid the agreed price, and left.

After a period of time the artist again visited the violin maker. Picking up a violin that was lying on the table, once again he drew the bow across the strings. This time he was charmed by the ravishing beauty of the tone. With astonishment he learned that this was the same violin he had broken to bits. The violin maker had painstakingly gathered up the pieces of the shattered instrument and, skillfully assembling them, had made again the broken violin. Now the beauty and brilliance of its tone met the exacting demands of the artist's ear.

What Is Meant by Brokenness?

One is not broken until all resentment and rebellion against God and man is removed. One who resents, takes offense, or retaliates against criticism and opposition or lack of appreciation is unbroken. All self-justification and self-defense betrays an unbroken spirit. All discontent and irritation with providential circumstances and situations reveals unbrokenness. Genuine brokenness usually requires years of crushing heartache and sorrow. Thus are self-will surrendered and deep degrees of yieldedness and submission developed, without which there is little agape love.

— *Brokenness Also Means Emptiness*

Watchman Nee said that God's great purpose in His dealing with us is to reduce us. This is because any confidence in one's own flesh is fatal to confidence and faith in God. Therefore, before God can release His own power to meet one's crisis need, He must bring that person to the end of himself.

Until one is broken, he is full of himself, his plans, his

ambitions, his value judgments. One is often so full of self that there is little room for more of God. Where this is true, God cannot enter in a deeper reality until there has been a divesting of selfish aims and goals, an utter self-emptying. Usually this requires disastrous failures, being "battered with the shocks of doom," complete disillusionment with one's flesh.

If thou couldst empty all thyself of self.
Like to a shell dishabited;
There might He find thee on the ocean shelf,
And say, "This is not dead,"
And fill thee with himself instead.

But thou art all replete with very thou,
And hast such shrewd activity,
That when He comes, He says, "This is enough
Unto itself; 'twere best let it be;
It is so small and full, there is no room for Me."

A Death to Self

Further illumination comes from George D. Watson's *A Deeper Death to Self:*

There is not only a death to sin, but in a great many things there is a deeper death to self—a crucifixion in detail, and in the minutia of life—after the soul has been sanctified. This deeper crucifixion to self is the unfolding and application of all the principles of self-renunciation which the soul agreed to in its full consecration. Job was a perfect man and dead to all sin; but in his great sufferings, he died to his own

religious life; died to his domestic affections; died to his theology; all his views of God's providence; he died to a great
many things that in themselves were not sin, but which hin-
dered his largest union with God.

Peter, after being sanctified and filled with the Spirit,
needed a special vision from heaven to kill him to his tradi-
tional theology and Jewish high churchism. The very largest
degrees of self-renunciation, crucifixion, and abandonment to
God, take place *after* the work of heart purity [emphasis
mine]. There are a multitude of things which are not sinful;
nevertheless our attachment to them prevents our greatest
fullness of the Holy Spirit and our amplest co-operation with
God. Infinite wisdom takes us in hand, and arranges to lead
us through deep, interior crucifixion to our fine parts, our
lofty reason, our brightest hopes, our cherished affections,
our religious views, our dearest friendships, our pious zeal,
our spiritual impetuosity, our narrow culture, our creeds and
churchism, our success, our religious experiences, our spiritual comforts; the crucifixion goes on until we are dead and
detached from all creatures, all saints, all thoughts, all hopes,
all plans, all tender heart yearnings, all preferences; dead to
all troubles, all sorrows, all disappointments; equally dead to
all praise or blame, success or failure, comforts or annoy-
ances; dead to all climates and nationalities; dead to all
desires but for *himself.* There are innumerable degrees of
interior crucifixion in these various lines. Perhaps not one
sanctified person in ten thousand ever reaches that degree of
death to self that Paul, and Madame Guyon, and similar
saints have reached.

In contradistinction to heart cleansing, this finer crucifixion of self is gradual; it extends through months and years;
the interior spirit is mortified over and over on the same
points, till it reaches a state of divine indifference to it. A
great host of believers have obtained heart purity, and yet for
a long time have gone through all sorts of "dying daily" to

self, before they found that calm, fixed union with the Holy Ghost which is the deep longing of the child of God. Again, in contradistinction to heart cleansing, which is by faith, *this deeper death to self is by suffering* [emphasis mine]. This is abundantly taught in Scripture, and confirmed by the furnace experiences of thousands.

Joseph was a sanctified man before being cast into prison; but there the iron entered into his soul (see Psalm 105:18), and by suffering he reached the highest death of self. There are literally scores of Scripture passages like Psalm 71:19–21, teaching that the upper ranges in the sanctified state are wrought out through suffering. Perhaps the most remarkable passage of the Word on this subject is in Romans, fifth chapter; the first verse teaches justification by faith, the second verse teaches full salvation by faith, and verses three to five teach a deeper death and fuller Holy Ghost life by tribulation.

When the soul undergoes this deeper death of self, it enters into a great wideness of spiritual comprehension and love; a state of almost uninterrupted prayer, of boundless charity for all people; of unutterable tenderness and broadness of sympathy; of deep, quiet thoughtfulness; of extreme simplicity of life and manners; and of deep visions into God and the coming ages. In this state of utter death to self, suffering, sorrow, pain and mortification of all kinds are looked upon with a calm, sweet indifference. Such a soul looks back over its heartbreaking trials, its scalding tears, its mysterious tribulations, with gentle subduedness, without regret, for it now sees God in every step of the way. Into such a soul the Holy Spirit pours the ocean current of His own life; its great work henceforth is to watch the monitions and movements of the Spirit within it, and to yield prompt, loving, unquestioning cooperation with Him. Such a soul has at last, in deed and in truth, reached the place where there is "none of self and all of Thee."

THE GREAT BUSINESS of LIFE

Explanation of the Mystery of Suffering

It is true that "whole, unbruised, unbroken men are of little use to God." In the here and now He cannot greatly use those who are hard, unloving, and self-centered. But God is not interested in brokenness primarily for its temporal value, great as that may be. His bride-elect is in training for the throne. She is in the school of suffering to learn agape love in order to qualify her for rulership in an economy where the law of love is supreme. This is why God is willing to take a lifetime to teach her love. No other cosmology can explain the mystery of suffering to which Peter says we are called. "Servants, be subject to your masters with all fear; not only to the good and gentle, but also to the froward. For this is thankworthy, if a man for conscience toward God endure grief, suffering wrongfully. For what glory is it, if, when ye be buffeted for your faults, ye shall take it patiently? but if, when ye do well, and suffer for it, ye take it patiently, this is acceptable with God. *For even hereunto were ye called:* because Christ also suffered for us, leaving us an example, that ye should follow his steps" (1 Peter 2:18–21 KJV, emphasis added).

— *Suffering—God's Grand Strategy*

Although brokenness is important in God's service on earth, God's primary purpose in permitting it is to get us prepared for his eternal assignment. The center of gravity of God's discipline is not time but eternity. Allowing God's discipline to wean us from vain ambition and selfishness increases agape love and transmutes our brokenness into eternal glory. Rejecting and refusing the painful circumstances that God planned for the crucifixion of self is to waste our sorrows.

All the unspeakable suffering of the saints, the combined sorrows, tragedies, heartaches, disappointments, the persecutions and martyrdoms in the history of the church universal from the first century to this present moment are justified only by taking eternity into consideration. All of them serve a purpose in the here and now, but their principal design is to teach agape love in preparation for eternal rulership. Suffering is God's grand strategy for creating rank in the bridehood for His eternal enterprise. It seems that only this can possibly justify earth's flood of sorrow. This illuminates Paul's statement to the Philippians: "For it has been granted to you on behalf of Christ not only to believe on him, but also to suffer for him" (Philippians 1:29). Also the statements of Peter: "Dear friends, do not be surprised at the painful trial you are suffering, as though something strange were happening to you. But rejoice that you participate in the sufferings of Christ, so that you may be overjoyed when his glory is revealed. If you are insulted because of the name of Christ, you are blessed, for the Spirit of glory and of God rests on you" (1 Peter 4:12–14). "And the God of all grace, who called you to his eternal glory in Christ, after you have suffered a little while, will himself restore you and make you strong, firm and steadfast" (1 Peter 5:10). It should also illuminate Paul's letter to the Thessalonians: "Therefore, among God's churches we boast about your perseverance and faith in all the persecutions and trials you are enduring. All this is evidence that God's judgment is right, and as a result you will be counted worthy of the kingdom of God, for which you are suffering" (2 Thessalonians 1:4–5).

— Qualified Through Suffering

In the Philippian passage cited above, Paul indicates that it is a privilege to suffer for Christ. This is difficult to understand apart from God's eternal purpose for us. While suffering may bear rich fruit in this life, that fruit is not always apparent and much of the time it seems insufficient to justify the suffering. If, as

Paul implies, it is a privilege to suffer for Christ, it must be related to the future order of things. If God's purpose in keeping a school of suffering here for His children is that of maturing us in agape love in preparation for rulership, then Paul's teaching that suffering is a privilege is rational. This also interprets his word to the Thessalonians concerning their persecutions and afflictions, which afflictions, he says, are "evidence that God's judgment is right." Why? That you may "be counted worthy of the kingdom of God, for which you are suffering." Paul is saying that without these persecutions and afflictions they could not qualify as meriting their rulership rank. This same concept also interprets and makes rational Peter's exhortation to "rejoice that you participate in the sufferings of Christ, so that you may be overjoyed when his glory is revealed . . . for the Spirit of glory and of God rests on you." There is simply no way to explain the biblical teaching on the glory of suffering and tribulation, except as an apprenticeship for the throne. No love without suffering. No rulership without love. Therefore, *only* if we suffer shall we reign with Him.

It is easy to doubt that one's present particular suffering qualifies to serve this high purpose. It may be of such a nature as to tempt one to disregard it and to feel that it is useless, or worse. Someday one may come to understand that the very sorrow that he thought most irrelevant was the one God used for His most glorious ends. This and this alone makes sense of the following lines:

> Things that hurt and things that mar
> Shape the man for perfect praise;
> Shock and strain and ruin are
> Friendlier than the smiling days.
> —John White Chadwick

Solomon's Temple

This principle is illustrated in the building of Solomon's temple. Every stone that went into that amazing structure was hewn to such exact specifications at the quarry site that each stone fitted perfectly into the place for which it was designed. "In building the temple, only blocks dressed at the quarry were used, and no hammer, chisel or any other iron tool was heard at the temple site while it was being built" (1 Kings 6:7).

Believers Are Living Stones

A. N. Hodgkin, in *Christ in All the Scriptures*, says, "All true believers in all ages are the living stones in that heavenly Temple, and God is preparing them in His quarry down here, amid the noise and tumult of earth, each for his place in His Temple above. Rugged and shapeless are the stones to begin with; no wonder that the blows of the hammer fall heavily, that the chisel is sharp, and the polishing severe before the stones are ready."[2]

At present we are not what we should be, neither are we what we shall be. But God does not work without a pattern or design. He knows what He is doing. There is nothing accidental about the providences that come into our lives. There is a Hand that is guiding and controlling these providences. There is a purpose running through all the events and circumstances. This purpose may not be evident to us, but there is an eye that always watches the pattern. It is God who fashions us.

> 'Tis the Master who holds the mallet,
> And day by day
> He is chipping whatever environs
> The form away;

Which, under His skillful cutting,
He means shall be
Wrought silently out to beauty
Of such degree
Of faultless and full perfection,
That angel eyes
Shall look on the finished labor
With new surprise,
That even His boundless patience
Could grave His own
Features upon such fractured
And stubborn stone.

—Anonymous

— *The Shaping of the Stones*

Hodgkin points out that when they are removed from the quarry, the stones are rugged and shapeless. Quarry stones are insensitive, but the "living stones" with which God is working are not. This means that God cannot shape without pain. *Where there is no pain, no shaping is achieved.* The tools He must use are sharp and abrasive. Quarry stones cannot resist, but the "living stones" may. When they do, their sorrow and pain is wasted. If God cannot shape one for his distinctive place in eternity without the use of affliction, may this not explain why many people continue to suffer physical illness in spite of long continued prayer for healing? If character is God's supreme aim in the universe and if character cannot be developed without pain, does this not illuminate the passage: "The Lord disciplines those he loves"? (Hebrews 12:6). Maybe God cannot get that special stone He needs for a particular place any other way. If so, is He to be denied, and are the person's sorrows wasted if he eventually qualifies for his unique place in that ethereal structure?

LEARNING AGAPE LOVE THROUGH FAMILY RELATIONSHIPS

According to our thesis, life is intended to be an education in agape love. All circumstances, whether of joy or sorrow, which are permitted to come to a child of God are for the purpose of teaching and maturing him in the love that is the prerequisite for rulership in the ultimate economy of God. This world is a laboratory in which those destined for the throne are learning by actual practice to be governed by the law of love, which principle they will administer in the ultimate social order.

Earth, the Sphere of Learning Love

There is only one place and time in which agape love can be learned and that is in the here and now, in a world just like this one. C. S. Lovett points out in his book *Unequally Yoked Wives*[1] that this character of agape love cannot be produced in heaven. This is a rather startling statement, but he says, "Heaven is no place to raise kids." There is no way to produce godliness there. The conditions required to bring people to spiritual maturity are not found there.

Superficially, one would think that heaven would be the ideal place to produce godly character. No more death, mourning, crying, or pain (Revelation 21:4). No more foes to cause fear. But, as Lovett points out, this means no more tension or strain. No more tests or temptations. No more opposition or hindrances. Total relaxation. Would not this kind of environment be ideal for the production of heavenly character? The answer is *by no means*. Dr. Lovett asks: "What happens to children when all stress is taken away? What happens when they are shielded from hardship, troubles, and oppositions of life? Do they grow, or merely stagnate?"

You know a lack of stress is no way to bring about strength of character. Therefore, heaven is no place to *bring* sons to maturity. *That* must be done here on earth in just the kind of a world God has placed us in. Lovett says, "A coddled child is fearful." And you know that a coddled saint is impossible.

Does this mean there will be no growth in heaven? No, it does not mean that. There the redeemed will live in an *entirely new order* (Revelation 21:4–5). In that order there may be many other stimulants to growth, and one of them will be praise and worship. Heaven is one grand paean of praise. In worship and praise of the infinitely lovely God one exercises the most sublime and divine dimensions of the human character. In this exercise, all of the most transcendent, ineffable, and godlike qualities of the being are activated and therefore enlarged. This growth process will be eternally accelerated in the celestial atmosphere and practice of praise and worship. There will be no need there for the stimulus of earthly sorrow, stress, and pain.

— *Purity Is Instantaneous*

A person receives purity of heart by an instantaneous act of faith in receiving the filling with the Holy Spirit (Acts 15:7–9; see also Acts 10:44–47). But maturity in agape love is another thing. Without purity of heart, maturity is impossible. Even with purity of heart, maturity is an extended process impossible apart from tribulation, pain, and stress. There is no shortcut. After many years, the apostle Paul testified that he had not yet attained the summit of maturity (Philippians 3:12–14).

— *Maturity Is a Lifetime Process*

Maturing into advanced states of Christian character and agape love is, of necessity, a lifetime operation. Take, for example, the grace of long-suffering. How is it acquired? Lovett answers: "By suffering a long time." But there is no suffering in heaven. Therefore, long-suffering cannot be acquired there.

What about patience? In my youth, some preachers of my acquaintance implied that the crisis experience of holiness brought instant patience, like instant coffee, instant grits, or other instant foods. But how are instant foods produced? By pre-cooking. They require the application of heat or pressure or both. It is the same with patience. There is no such thing as instant patience. Advanced degrees of patience (which is only a by-product or manifestation of agape love) are gained by enduring one anxiety after another. But there is no anxiety in heaven, therefore patience cannot be learned there.

Consider the grace of forgiveness, another manifestation of agape love. Does one not have to be hurt or amended before he can forgive? Then high degrees of the grace of forgiveness are developed only by being hurt again and again and again. But there are no hurts or offenses in heaven, so forgiveness cannot be learned there.

Life Is a Laboratory

Therefore, a lifetime of sorrow, anguish, and disappointment is required to transform one into the lofty likeness of the Lord, to lead him into advanced degrees of maturity in Christlikeness and agape love. And these things are not found in heaven. Earth alone provides the kind of situations that produce mature sainthood. Here and here alone can one be tested by sorrow, frustration, and life-changing stresses. It is important to remember that this life is a laboratory, an apprenticeship in which God is teaching His children agape love in preparation for rulership.

Home Is a Microcosm

The home is the logical place to begin a course in learning agape love. Dr. Lovett says, "Marriage and the home is the center of all life on earth. . . . It is a complete laboratory with all of the stresses and strains, trials and pressures, packed under one roof. . . . Everything needed to produce Christlikeness in us can be found in the home." In other words, the home is a microcosm or miniature world, a facsimile of the world at large. The home, with its environment of stress and strain, is the best place to learn agape love. That is one of the reasons why God ordained the home, why He "set the solitary in families" (Psalm 68:6). Lovett said, "Marriage is the most stressful fact of life. If the whole of life is stress, then marriage is the center of stress."

— *Newlyweds Are Often Self-Centered*

J. R. Miller said,

> No two lives, however thorough their former acquaintance may have been, however long they may have moved together in society or mingled in the closer and more intimate relations of a ripening friendship, ever find themselves perfectly in harmony on their marriage day. It is only when that mysterious blending begins after marriage, which no language can explain, that each finds so much in the other that was never discovered before. . . . There are incompatibilities that were never dreamed of till they were revealed in the attrition of domestic life.[2]

There may be exceptions, but most newlyweds have not yet learned the true meaning of unselfishness. They may be saved, sanctified, or filled with the Holy Spirit, and still be unconsciously self-centered. One of God's main purposes in ordaining marriage and the home is not primarily for pleasure, as is ordinarily supposed, but to decentralize the self, to teach agape love. The stresses of marriage and the home are designed to produce brokenness, to wean one from self-centeredness, and to produce the graces of sacrificial love and gentleness.

Because so few people understand the nature and purpose of marriage, when unexpected stresses and strains develop they are tempted to feel that they have made a mistake and perhaps have married the wrong person. The next step is to seek a way of escape by one means or another, sometimes through a professional marriage counselor or, more often, the divorce court.

— A Spiritual Problem

If the marriage counselor is a professional and works for pay, his services, based as they generally are on Freudian principles, could be worthless, or worse. Except where there is organic difficulty, the root of all conflicts in the home is not mental, but spiritual. Psychology and psychiatry are often totally irrelevant. *A spiritual problem always has a spiritual cause and requires a spiritual solution.* Many counselors, even some who are Christians, have been so influenced by Freud that they are totally unprepared to deal with a spiritual problem in a scriptural way. Many spiritually discerning persons are quite convinced that psychiatry is Satan's substitute for the biblical remedy for disturbed relationships. Many psychiatrists seek to help the person under stress by relieving him of personal responsibility for his difficulty— which only compounds the trouble. The origin of the conflict, except in organic cases, where there may be a chemical imbalance, is almost invariably spiritual. The ego is inflated. Love is lacking. This is entirely a spiritual problem. The way out is *not* through separation or divorce. That would frustrate God's purpose and only aggravate the problems.

— Sacrificial Love

If one or both of the persons involved is born again, God's design is that each will teach the other agape love. And this is not easy. The life of nature and of self dies hard. But if even one partner understands that life is for learning love and that the home is the arena where it is best taught and learned, a beginning in dealing with self-centeredness may be made. If the couple can comprehend that neither life nor marriage is made primarily for pleasure but for learning sacrificial love, they may not waste their sorrows.

— Horizontal Versus Vertical

Trouble in a horizontal relationship is always the result of trouble in the vertical relationship—with God. Somewhere self-will has taken over. Antagonism toward a mate is first of all antagonism toward God. Lack of love for a marriage partner is really lack of love for God: "Dear friends, let us love one another, for love comes from God. Everyone who loves has been born of God and knows God. Whoever does not love does not know God, because God is love. If we love one another, God lives in us and his love is made complete in us. If anyone says, 'I love God,' yet hates his brother, he is a liar. For anyone who does not love his brother, whom he has seen, cannot love God, whom he has not seen" (1 John 4:7–8, 12, 20).

— The Right to Surrender Rights

When either marriage partner gives as the excuse for separation that love for the other person is gone, the trouble is not primarily between the couple themselves but between one or both of them and God. When at least one of them gets really right with God, he no longer stubbornly insists on his rights or having things his way. Someone has said that the only right a Christian has is the right to give up his rights. This agrees with the Sermon on the Mount, Matthew 5 and 6. The partner closest to God will almost always be the first to yield. Love for God will enable him to surrender his prerogatives and accept self-crucifixion. If he or she is not willing to do this, it is because his love for God is deficient. Refusal to suffer loss for Christ's sake is really rebellion against God.

— Repentance and Restitution

If this is the situation, no amount of professional counseling or psychiatric treatment will change it until the spiritual problem is solved. It is doubtful if a non-Christian counselor or psychiatrist understands this and can be of any help. Help will come only when one or both of the partners understands that life is for learning agape love in preparation for rulership in eternity and they are willing to suffer the pain involved in adjustment and forgiveness. Repentance toward God for any lack of love and restitution toward each other will bring the growth in love that God intends. Paul gives instruction in Ephesians 5:21–23 concerning submission, which is so vital to growth in love: "Submit to one another out of reverence for Christ. Wives, submit to your husbands as to the Lord. For the husband is the head of the wife as Christ is the head of the church, his body, of which he is the Savior." Peter also emphasizes this principle in 1 Peter 5:5–6: "Young men, in the same way be submissive to those who are older. All of you, clothe yourselves with humility toward one another, because, 'God opposes the proud but gives grace to the humble.' Humble yourselves, therefore, under God's mighty hand, that he may lift you up in due time." Unwillingness to accept these principles of submission will result not only in increased heartache and pain but also in the waste of one's sorrows.

— An Insecure Foundation

Much of marriage counseling is oriented toward the here and now. The primary goal is to heal the endangered marriage in the interest of the present happiness of the partners. This is very natural. But so long as the pair suffers with the illusion that the main purpose of life and wedlock is blissful pleasure and happiness, the foundation of their marriage is insecure. Until they understand that life and marriage is an apprenticeship for the practice of agape love in preparation for rulership where the law of love is supreme, they are in danger of eternal loss. If they spend their years in regrets, disappointments, and recriminations, they have wasted their sorrows. If they accept one another as God's disciplinary agents to bring each other into increasing selflessness and growing agape love, they may not only find greater happiness here but also achieve "an eternal glory that far outweighs them all" in the hereafter.

— A Tragedy of Our Times

All of the efforts by psychologists and psychiatrists to bring about a reorientation and reintegration of personalities in marriage without dealing with the basic spiritual problem are in vain. It is sad to see the church and the ministry forsaking the biblical way of soul healing for a massive satanic delusion. It is one of the most lamentable tragedies of recent history. "'Be appalled at this, O heavens, and shudder with great horror,' declares the LORD. 'My people have committed two sins: They have forsaken me, the spring of living water, and have dug their own cisterns, broken cisterns that cannot hold water'" (Jeremiah 2:12–13). Nowhere is this truer than in the professional mental health programs operated under the supervision of religious groups.

— A Professional Opinion

This is the opinion not only of a layman but also of some highly respected professionals. In chapters 6 and 7 of his book *The Crisis in Psychiatry and Religion,*[3] Dr. O. Hobart Mowrer, research psychologist at the University of Illinois and former president of the American Psychological Association, has strongly reproved the Christian ministry for referring the mentally disturbed members of their congregations to psychiatrists when the ministers of the Word of God alone have the answers to these kinds of problems.

— An Atheistic Philosophy

It is a sorrowful reflection upon Him who said, "'Come to me, all you who are weary and burdened, and I will give you rest'" (Matthew 11:28), when His servants and representatives become so undiscerning, confused, and powerless as to seek the assistance of a profession that is predominantly atheistic, deterministic, and evolutionary in its philosophy. Furthermore, a large segment of the profession has repudiated biblical principles of morality, attributing much mental disturbance to over-conscientiousness in efforts to live by those principles.

— Seduction As Therapy

An article in *The Atlanta Constitution,* January 26, 1976, reveals the widespread practice by professional counselors of using so-called sexual therapy as a treatment in mental illness. Under the headline "Seduction in Therapy Called a Major Problem" the dispatch reads: "One of the most pressing problems facing the rapidly expanding field of sex therapy today is the practice of therapists who sometimes seduce patients seeking cures to sexual problems. . . ."

A lengthy discussion of sexual relations between therapists and patients was led by Yale University psychiatrist Fritz Redich, who said such sex with clients is frequent among many types of professionals.

In a recent newspaper article, a psychiatrist is quoted as openly admitting this practice and saying that he gets a weekly fee of fifty dollars for his "professional" service in one instance. That makes him a gigolo or male prostitute masquerading as a therapist.

Psychoanalysis Is Not a Science

Although, according to the above dispatch, the practice is frequent, the charge is not being made here that it is representative of the profession as a whole. While there are some professing Christian psychiatrists, it seems a misnomer to this writer. According to some recognized authorities, psychiatry is not a science, even though it poses as one. It is called a faith, not logic.[4] While the profession seems to proliferate, some well-known writers call mental health a myth and identify neurosis as "not a medical problem but a moral conflict."[5]

— *Integrity Therapy*

Dr. Mowrer has sponsored a new approach to mental health problems that is called "Integrity Therapy." It boils down to the biblical method of healing: repentance, restitution, forgiveness, and full transparency with all parties concerned, leading to a right relationship with God and one another. A right vertical relationship is the secret of a satisfying horizontal relationship. Perfect transparency with God and one another is the remedy for stress in personal relationships.

— A Professional's Advice

Author-psychologist Lee R. Steiner's remarks should give pause to the minister who is, consciously or unconsciously, enamored with the psychiatric approach to mental health and spiritual problems: "It is my impression from twenty years of study of where people take their troubles and why they seek out the sources they do, that the ministry makes a tremendous mistake when it swaps what it has for psychosomatic dressing. Through the ages, ministry has been the force that has at least attempted to keep morality alive. It would be a pity if, in one of the areas of greatest moral crisis, the clergy should suddenly abandon its strength for something that has no validity, no roots, and no value. It is my impression that they would do far better to cling to what they have. Judaism has endured for almost six thousand years, Christianity for about two thousand. Where will psychoanalysis be in twenty-five years? I predict it will take its place along with phrenology and mesmerism."[6]

The Only Remedy

To reemphasize: When a home or marriage is threatened, the basic cause is spiritual. Therefore, the remedy is spiritual, not psychological. Stresses and strains are certain to come. When the parties accept them as God's way of teaching them agape love in preparation for the throne in eternity, welcoming them by offering the sacrifice of praise (Hebrews 13:15), domestic conflicts may be resolved and transmuted into future glory.

Marital Unfaithfulness

These are hazardous days in which almost all cherished values are crumbling. The world is adrift in a sea of uncertainty and doubt. Society is in a state of ethical shock. The social order is disintegrating. Moral chaos thrives. Sexual anarchy prevails. Mass insanity threatens. This disintegration of the social order is an evidence of an invasion of sex-oriented demons, driving up the divorce rate and destroying the institution of marriage, the home, and the family. But God can use this very situation to develop agape love in His bride-elect.

— Overruling Moral Failure

One of the greatest opportunities for learning agape love is presented to the Christian man or woman whose mate has become the victim of promiscuous sex demons. There is no greater temptation to bitterness than the unfaithfulness of a marriage partner. Thousands are being caught in this maelstrom of moral permissiveness induced by the "new morality" and the relaxation of moral standards it promotes. Mrs. Billy Graham has been quoted as saying that if God continues to spare our decadent morals, He should apologize to Sodom and Gomorrah. Husbands and wives may not realize it, but this very situation offers an unprecedented opportunity to enhance eternal rank by learning a deeper dimension of agape love. If one succumbs to resentment, self-pity, and revenge, *he has wasted his sorrow*. But if one understands that grace can overrule this sorrow and use it for teaching agape love, he may be able to use his unspeakable anguish for everlasting gain. Not many do, but some have triumphed.

An Affirmation

For those who are having any sort of domestic difficulty, the following affirmative prayer is suggested:

> Father, I offer the sacrifice of praise for my mate just as he (she) is because you have permitted him (her) to be this

way and have brought us together in a marriage relationship.
I know that you are able and therefore I know that you are
working through him (her) as he (she) is to bring your purposes to pass, overruling his (her) spiritual, character, and
personality limitations for your glory. Amen.

Try practicing this affirmation at every moment of irritation
or injury for six months and see what happens.

The Generation Gap

Although this is the day of the so-called generation gap, it is as
old as Adam and his son Cain, and Noah and his son Ham.
However, Freudian psychology and the school of psychiatry it
spawned has greatly aggravated and enlarged the breach
between parents and children. The resulting alienation and the
rejection of moral and spiritual ideals by the younger generation
is capable of producing the most agonizing suffering. This is a
problem of massive proportions. The fact that no parent is perfect and so may be partially responsible for the alienation does
not assuage the grief. The wounds opened by filial ingratitude
are only aggravated by the blighting effects of this alienation
upon the loved one himself, who is dearer than life. King David
has many brothers and sisters who join him in his soliloquy over
a son who reaped as he sowed and brought crushing sorrow to
his parents. But according to the apostle Paul, even this devastating grief may be transmuted into "an eternal glory that far
outweighs them all" if it is allowed to work in the parent that
deeper dimension of agape love that is redemptive. Out of the
agony of rejection a parent may discover self-centeredness of
which he was unaware. By sincere repentance and self-
repudiation he may grow in sacrificial love that is healing,
restorative, and eternally rewarding. This may be one reason
why God permits the agonies of the generation gap. The

resulting crushing sorrows should not be wasted. The cost of learning to love may be high, but God considers no price too great. By these sorrows He is training His bride-elect to live by the law of love.

10

LEARNING AGAPE LOVE THROUGH WRONGFUL SUFFERING

To recapitulate: If all born-again believers are in apprenticeship for rulership, and if a lofty dimension of agape love is the supreme qualification for high rank and authority in that eternal social order toward which the universe is moving, and if a high dimension of agape love cannot be achieved without suffering, could this explain why God permits many who seek healing to suffer on, even for a lifetime?

The Discipline of Delay

If God healed everyone immediately, where would be the opportunity for character training? If God delivered everyone from conflict, oppression, and opposition at the first call, where would be the opportunity for the perseverance that creates character? If tribulation were lifted at the first cry, where would be the chance for exercise in patience that issues in heavenly character, the chief ingredient of which is agape love? If Jesus' human experience in leadership could not be perfected without suffering, can our training for heavenly rulership be perfected without it? The answer is, probably not.

How Pure Evil Is Transformed

The question is: How are "these light and momentary troubles," which seem unbearable and endless to us, to be transmuted into that "eternal glory that far outweighs them all"? One's afflictions can be made to work for him only by a correct subjective attitude. To many, it is a mystery how a *subjective* attitude toward an *objective* situation can so modify its effect that pure evil is transformed into a sublime dimension of good.

The Eternal Essence of Any Situation

Consider the following: *Nothing that comes to us from any source can injure us unless it causes us to have a wrong attitude.* It is our response that blesses or harms. Amy Carmichael said that the eternal essence of a thing is not in the thing itself but in one's reaction to it. The distressing situation will pass, but our reaction toward it will leave a moral and spiritual impression in our character that is eternal. This being true, all that God permits to come to us must be working for our good unless we allow it to separate us from God. "The only real calamity in life is to lose one's faith in God" (Maclaren). The circumstances and situations that confront us are beyond our control; we can do nothing about them. But with the help of God we can control our reaction, our subjective attitude. That is entirely within our own jurisdiction. If, because of the apparent evil that has come, we allow ourselves to fall into an attitude of self-pity, frustration, and rebellion toward others and God, our character deteriorates and we are wasting our sorrow. But when we accept the advice of the apostle James, everything is different. "Consider it pure joy, my brothers, whenever you face trials of many kinds, because you know that the testing of your faith develops perseverance. Perseverance must finish its work so that you may be mature and complete, not lacking anything" (James 1:2–4). This is in harmony with Paul's statement in Romans 5:3–5: "We also rejoice in our sufferings, because we know that suffering produces perseverance; perseverance, character; and character, hope. And hope does not disappoint us, because God has poured out his love into our hearts by the Holy Spirit, whom he has given us." According to this passage, the ultimate result of rejoicing in tribulation is agape love shed abroad in the heart. This is supreme gain.

— Blessed Be Suffering

If God cannot develop the quality of character that is needed for rulership in the ages to come without suffering, then should not our attitude be "Blessed be suffering"? Rank in heaven will be determined not by magnetic personality, glittering talents, towering intellect, or other coveted endowments, but by the depth and quality of one's love. Earth, with its sorrow, heartbreak, disappointments, and pain, is the only place, and this life is the only time, when this love can be developed. This love is the coin, currency, and legal tender of heaven. It can be developed only in the school of suffering. Before suffering has done its benevolent work, how hard, harsh, arrogant, cutting, overbearing, tactless, impatient, even mean, many of us have been. How often we have ridden roughshod over the legitimate feelings, sensibilities, and opinions of others. These are all traits of self-centeredness. Only by suffering, oftentimes severely, are these unlovely characteristics and dispositions softened and sweetened. This is why God has to take many of us through refining fires, why many must be battered until they are bruised, broken, and made utterly empty of themselves. A hymnwriter wrote:

> Oh, to be nothing, nothing;
> Simply to lie at His feet:
> A broken and emptied vessel
> For the Master's use made meet.

Job's Decentralization

Before he suffered, Job knew God by reputation only. Afterward he said, "Now my eyes have seen you." Before his suffering was complete he argued with God, actually accusing Him of wrongdoing. (Read Job 10.) Afterward he said, "I despise myself and repent in dust and ashes" (Job 42:6). Job's experience is an illustration of 1 Peter 4:1: "He who has suffered in his body is done with sin." God testified that Job was a holy man, yet there were traits of self-centeredness of which, at first, he was totally unaware and which could be spotlighted and removed only by deep affliction.

The proof that out of Job's long trial of severe sorrow came a new dimension of agape love is the fact that he was willing to pray for his severe critics and they were spared the Lord's judgment. To accept criticism sweetly, without retaliation or resentment, is an evidence of growth in love. This is one reason why Jesus said to "love your enemies"—because they afford us the opportunity to grow in agape love, the insignia of rank in eternity (Matthew 5:44–48).

On-the-Job Training

All of God's discipline and training is directed toward increasing and perfecting love. All adversity, whatever its character or magnitude, is permitted for this purpose. God uses temporal circumstances, personality clashes, personal hostilities, unjust criticism, financial reverses, poverty, physical affliction, frailty, pain, and even old age as on-the-job training for the exercise and development of agape love in us. This training is not primarily for temporal value and advantage, since life's day is often nearing its end before one learns the deeper lessons of love, but because it is the legal tender of eternity. We need to be often. reminded that we are in apprenticeship here in life's school of

suffering to learn love primarily as eternal equipment and qualification for rulership in heaven.

Furthermore, this means that all hindrances to the believer's
deliverance, right up to total glorification, is on the human side.
Enoch proved, verified, and confirmed this principle by appro-
priating faith for glorification (Genesis 5:24; Hebrews 11:5).
Enoch's experience proves that there is a legal basis for full
deliverance in this life from every result of the fall for every
child of God. If one fallen man is legally delivered (see chapter
4), then potentially all must be. This is the only explanation for
Enoch's experience.

— *Affliction and Character Development*

Since Enoch's experience was the result of a perfect faith, all
failure to obtain full deliverance from any result of the fall must
be the failure of faith. And failure of faith in well-taught believers is the result of one thing: defect in Christian character.
Therefore, all infirmities, sickness, and disease that remain in a
knowledgeable believer's life must be related to character development alone. Alexander Maclaren, believing that every affliction comes with a message from the heart of God, said that if
we knew ourselves better, and could see as God sees, we could
trace all of our unanswered prayers to defects in our own Christian character.

Because these things are true, all afflictions that are not
removed in answer to prayer should be understood as God's way
of disciplining character into the pattern of godlikeness that is
fitting one specifically for his particular role in the ages to come.

— *Purposeful Sorrow*

All that God permits to come to the members of His bride
is intended to mature them in love—necessary in their

administrative capacity as "kings and priests." Life on earth in a fallen social order is the only situation in which this love has any chance for practice and development. This explains why Paul said, "If we endure, we will also reign with him" (2 Timothy 2:12) and "We share in his sufferings in order that we may also share in his glory" (Romans 8:17).

— *Purposeful Tribulation*

It has been pointed out that as soon as a person is born again he enters apprenticeship for rulership in that social order where the law of agape love is supreme. Since tribulation is necessary for the decentralization of the self and the development of agape love, Paul says we are to glory in it, and only to the extent to which we glory in it does tribulation serve us and achieve God's purpose. If we fight against it by self-pity and rebellion, by murmuring and complaining, by accusing God of wrongdoing, we are wasting our sorrows.

Called to Unjust Suffering

None of the things—not even the worst—that come to a child of God are ever accidental. They are controlled experiments intended to give him opportunity to exercise and learn agape love. No one in his right mind would count it a privilege to suffer wrongfully unless he sees it as an opportunity to increase his rank in the eternal kingdom. God must have had this in mind when He inspired Peter to write: "Slaves, submit yourselves to your masters with all respect, not only to those who are good and considerate, but also to those who are harsh. For it is commendable if a man bears up under the pain of unjust suffering because he is conscious of God. But how is it to your credit if you receive a beating for doing wrong and endure it? But if you suffer for doing good and you endure it, this is commendable before God. To this you were called, because Christ suffered for you, leaving you an example, that you should follow in his steps" (1 Peter 2:18–21). Understanding that this is God's way of enabling one to increase his eternal rank can hold one steady under unjust suffering. May this not explain why God permits persecution and martyrdom as well as the injustices and heartbreaking situations He allows in the lives of all saints everywhere? "For it has been granted to you on behalf of Christ not only to believe on him, but also to suffer for him" (Philippians 1:29).

— Trouble Is a Trust

It is difficult to receive injury from others without feeling resentment. It is hard to suffer wrongfully without becoming cynical and bitter. It is a problem to keep love in the heart through all unkindness, ingratitude, misunderstanding, injuries, abuses, and griefs. God may permit great personal inequity to come to you. Trouble is a trust, and for this reason you should "Consider it pure joy . . . whenever you face trials of many kinds, because you know that the testing of your faith develops perseverance. Perseverance must finish its work so that you may be mature and complete" (James 1:2–4). "In this you greatly rejoice, though now for a little while you may have suffered grief in all kinds of trials. These have come so that your faith—of greater worth than gold, which perishes though refined by fire—may be proved genuine and may result in praise [enhanced rank], glory and honor when Jesus Christ is revealed" (1 Peter 1:6–7).

— A Fertilizer of Character

Notice that trials of many kinds issue in maturity (of love), and grief in all kinds of trials results in praise, glory, and honor when Jesus Christ is revealed. If a child of God could actually see into the future and fully visualize the exaltation that the school of suffering is creating for him, it would be easier to glory in the tribulation, which often, instead, immerses him in deep depression. Austin Phelps said, "Suffering is a wonderful fertilizer to the roots of character. This is the only thing we can carry into eternity. . . . To gain the most of it and the best of it, is the object of probation." Cortland Myers said, "Someday, God is going to reveal the fact to every Christian that the very principles they now rebel against have been the instruments He used in perfecting their characters and molding them into perfection, polished stones for His great building yonder."

"Sometime"

If we could push ajar the gates of life,
And stand within, and all God's working see,
We might interpret all this doubt and strife,
And for each mystery could find a key.

But not today. Then be content, poor heart;
God's plans, like lilies pure and white, unfold.
We must not tear the close-shut leaves apart—
Time will reveal the calyxes of gold.

And if, through patient toil, we reach the land
Where tired feet, with sandals loosed, may rest,
When we shall clearly know and understand,
I think that we shall say, "God knew best."
—Charles E. Orr

God's Slow Work

In his writings, Dr. J. R. Miller tells of a young mother whose two small children were taken from her in death in one day. She collapsed under the burden of her grief. One day through her tears she sobbed, "I don't see why God made me." Her aunt, who was caring for her and was wiser in the ways of the Lord, said, "Dear, you are not yet made. God is making you now." God takes one as he is and spends a lifetime fashioning him into His image.

Behind my life the Weaver stands,
    And works His wondrous will.
I leave it in His all-wise hands,
    And trust His perfect skill;
Should mystery enshroud His plan,
    And my short sight be dim,
I will not try the whole to scan,
    But leave each thread with Him.

Nor till the loom is silent,
    And the shuttles cease to fly,
Shall God unfold the pattern
    And explain the reason why
The dark threads were as needful
    (In the Master's skillful hand)
As the threads of gold and silver
    In the pattern which He planned.

—*Unknown*

This Is Not the Devil's World

"This is not a world of chance—there is no chance anywhere. This is not the devil's world. All the universe is under the Father's personal sway. Our adversary is a created being under God's control. The divine hand is active in all the affairs of earth. 'My Father worketh hitherto and I work.' In all that He permits—joy, sorrow, success, failure, hope and fear, pleasure and pain, He is making us.

"But God does not make us all at once. The process is a long one, running through all the years of life, how many soever those years may be. God begins making us when we are born into the world, and His work in us goes on continuously unto the end of our days. There is never an hour when some new touch is not given to our life, some new line marked in our character. . . . Always God is on the field and He works in and through all experiences. . . . There is nothing accidental in any of the providences that come into our lives."[1]

It is important to remember, as Dr. Miller says, that Satan is a created being. He is *not* Lord of the universe, because he is a part of creation. Whatever authority he won through Adam's fall was lost at Calvary. In Matthew 28:18 Jesus said, "All authority in heaven and on earth has been given to *me*." Predicated upon the victory of Calvary, Jesus delegated, in Luke 10:19, that authority to His disciples and through them to the church. Until Satan's final incarceration (Revelation 20:10) and the subsequent marriage supper of the Lamb, God is using Satan for His own purposes to teach the bride-elect the technique of overcoming (Revelation 3:21) and a deeper dimension of agape love.

When one understands that agape love is the insignia of rank in that social order called the kingdom of God, and that this love is cultivated only in the school of suffering, he can better appreciate the truth expressed in these lines:

Sometime, when all life's lessons have been learned,
    And sun and stars forevermore have set,
The things which our weak judgments here have spurned,
    The things o'er which we grieved with lashes wet,
Will flash before us, out of life's dark night,
    As stars shine most in deeper tints of blue,
And we shall see how all God's plans were right,
    And what we thought reproof, was love most true.

—Sarah C. Follett

LEARNING AGAPE LOVE THROUGH LIFE'S FAILURES

No Price Is Too Great

God will go to any length to mold and mature us in His love. He considers no price too great because He knows the glory that lies ahead.

When God wants to drill a man,
* And thrill a man,*
And skill a man
* To play the noblest part;*
When He yearns with all His heart
* To create so great and bold a man*
That all the world shall be amazed,
* Watch His methods, watch His ways!*
How He ruthlessly perfects
* Whom He royally elects!*
How He hammers him and hurts him,
* And with mighty blows converts him*
Into trial shapes of clay, which
* Only God understands;*

While his tortured heart is crying
And he lifts beseeching hands!
How he bends but never breaks
When his good He undertakes;
How He uses whom He chooses,
And with every purpose fuses him;
By every act induces him
To try his splendor out—
God knows what He's about.

—Angela Morgan (adapted)

The writer of these lines apparently was thinking mostly of God's training for time on earth. But God's purpose in taking a man through a course of severe discipline as described in this poem is to prepare him for the eternal kingdom. "For the common deeds of the common day are ringing bells in the far away," that is, in eternity.

The Tip of the Iceberg

Many excellent writers justify suffering on the basis of its value in time and the contribution it makes to character and the kingdom in the here and now. There is much to be said for this viewpoint. Volumes have been written concerning the value of tribulation and sorrow in the building of character and the fashioning of a meritorious lifestyle. In one of his books, J. R. Miller has expressed this faith beautifully: "We do not know how much we owe to suffering. Many of the richest blessings that have come down to us from the past are the fruit of sorrow and pain."[1]

In another place, Dr. Miller said, "The world's greatest blessings have come out of its greatest sorrows. Goethe is reported to have said, 'I never had an affliction which did not turn into a poem.' It is probable that the best music and poetry in all literature had a similar origin. It has been said that 'poets learn in suffering what they write in song.' Nothing really worthwhile comes without pain and cost. When we read some rich passage in Christian literature that just fits, we have no idea what it cost the writer in suffering to learn the truths set forth in those passages." Another has said that "sorrows come to stretch out spaces in the heart for joy."

These are beautiful thoughts. It is true that even here and now sorrow has its compensations. Many of these may be realized before the close of life's day. The discipline of sorrow pays rich dividends in the present. But those rewards are as the tip of an iceberg when compared to the glory that shall be revealed. The primary purpose of sanctified affliction will not become apparent until the bride is on the throne with her Bridegroom. Then and only then will the meaning of Paul's glorious prophecy be revealed: "Our light and momentary troubles are achieving for us an eternal glory that far outweighs them all." Do not try to fathom the effect and purpose of affliction now. Eternity alone will unveil its grandeur.

The Bride-Elect— An Object Lesson in the Universe

We do not know the nature of God's eternal enterprise, but we know that it is immeasurably great. "No eye has seen, no ear has heard, no mind has conceived what God has prepared for those who love him" (1 Corinthians 2:9). We also know that the church is the central factor, the chief personality, the ranking character, the stellar celebrity in that eternal kingdom. "His intent was that now, *through the church*, the manifold wisdom of

God should be made known to the rulers and authorities in the heavenly realms" (Ephesians 3:10, emphasis added).

What is the content of God's "manifold wisdom" that He is seeking to make known to the "rulers and authorities in the heavenly realms" *through the church?* Since love is the law of the universe, and since the church is in the school of suffering to learn love, that "manifold wisdom" must consist of a sublime dimension of agape love.

Because God plans to use the church, the bride-elect, in eternity to express His love-nature to the principalities and powers, to all the intelligences of the universe, this is doubtless a principal reason He takes such pains to teach her individual members deep dimensions of agape love. There must be some things about God's love and the plan of salvation that are a mystery to the angels, as suggested in 1 Peter 1:12: "Even angels long to look into these things." Evidently God plans to use the church to educate and enlighten the inhabitants of His ever-expanding celestial empire. Hallelujah!

The Centrality of the Church

"For by him all things were created: things in heaven and on earth, visible and invisible, whether thrones or [political] powers or rulers or authorities; all things were created by him and for him. He is before all things, and in him all things hold together. *And he is the head of the body, the church"* (Colossians 1:16–18). This last statement is the clincher. It is reinforced by Ephesians 1:22, "And God placed all things under his feet and appointed him to be the head over everything *for the church,* which is his body, *the fullness of him* who fills everything in every way." He is "head over everything *for* the church." All the divine enterprise revolves around the church. Think of it! The church is closer to the seat of universal power than all the vast array of current and future thrones, principalities, powers, rulers, and authorities in the universe (1 Corinthians 3:21–23). In fact, the church is so close to the seat of supreme authority that she is a part of it as His body and is to be enthroned with Him. Therefore, God will go to any length necessary to prepare His individual members for their exalted positions.

— "The Worker Rather Than the Work"

This is why He will go to such pains to produce utter brokenness, compassion, and ultimately, agape love. For instance, sometimes God permits one of His servants a large measure of spiritual success for many years. He seems to lead a charmed life. Every effort he makes is prospered and blessed. Then God permits him to be overwhelmed with seeming disaster. He is utterly broken. A work of God, under his hand, perishes with apparent loss to the cause. It is a mystery. But God has a reason.

The Success of Failure

Sometimes, to suffer failure is the only way one can learn selflessness. Sometimes the suffering of adversity, catastrophic disaster, and utter loss is necessary to produce the meekness, compassion, and humility without which one may remain unqualified for his future rank. Ill-health may be followed by financial disaster, loss of reputation, or personal tragedy. If failure works better than success to prepare a man for rulership, you can be sure that God loves him too much to shield him at the expense of his "eternal glory." God seems to endorse the theme "the worker rather than the work," because God has eternal values in view. Oswald Chambers says, "Why shouldn't we go through heartbreaks? If through a broken heart God can bring His purposes to pass in the world, then thank Him for breaking your heart."[2]

The Temporal Versus the Eternal

The temptation of many gifted religious leaders is to aim and work for temporal success, a kingdom of their own here and now. The present strong, almost exclusive, emphasis upon the positive by some very successful religious entrepreneurs is an example.[3] The writer fears that some of these men will have to see their work shattered and broken by failure and defeat if they are to share that "eternal glory" that Paul writes about. An unknown writer has voiced this viewpoint in the following lines:

While the voice of the world shouts its chorus,
Its paean for those who have won;
While the trumpet is sounding triumphant,
And high to the breeze and the sun,
Glad banners are waving, hands clapping,
And hurrying feet thronging
After the laurel-crowned victors,
I stand on the field of defeat
In the shadow with those who are fallen and wounded and dying,
And there chant a requiem low—
Place my hand on their pain-knitted brow,
Breathe a prayer, hold a hand that is helpless,
And whisper, "They only the victory win,
Who have fought the good fight,
And have vanquished the demon that tempts us within."

Mixed Motives

How many of us have mixed motives of which we are totally unaware until God permits purifying adversity. That demon within us is vain ambition, human energy, and uncrucified flesh.

God will go to any length to exorcise it, even to the extent of allowing failure to an apparently spiritual work. He is working for the man's eternal rank and His own eternal glory.

"By the grace God has given me, I laid a foundation as an expert builder, and someone else is building on it. But each one should be careful how he builds. For no one can lay any foundation other than the one already laid, which is Jesus Christ. If any man builds on this foundation using gold, silver, costly stones, wood, hay or straw, his work will be shown for what it is, because the Day will bring it to light. It will be revealed with fire, and the fire will test the quality of each man's work. If what he has built survives, he will receive his reward. If it is burned up, he will suffer loss; he himself will be saved, but only as one escaping through the flames" (1 Corinthians 3:10–15).

The Worship of Success

This is a day when not only the secular world worships success but many church leaders are guilty as well. Success seems to be the god of some leaders of great ecclesiastical enterprises. John Henry Newman, who articulated this spiritual vice in the hymn "Lead, Kindly Light," has many brothers and sisters. He wrote:

I loved the garish day, and, spite of fears,
Pride ruled my will:
Remember not past years.

Only after a mighty breaking may some of us see our fault. It may take a lifetime for God to disillusion us with success, purify our motives, and mature us in agape love. It often seems that when some people have reached that maturity in love which renders them most effective, just when they have arrived at the peak of their usefulness, God takes them to heaven. Many wonder why, when a person seems most ready for fruitful service, God summons him home. This makes no sense unless God's purpose in life is not primarily for service in time but for God's eternal enterprises. God has used the circumstances of life, whether of joy or sorrow, pleasure or pain, success or failure, to mature us for our exalted role in His future kingdom. When God has achieved this, there is little point in leaving us here any longer.

To Live Life Over Again

Many times as a person nears the end of his days he becomes more conscious of eternal truths. In the light of passing years, his perspective has changed. As the evening shadows lengthen, his system of values is revised. The things he once so highly prized now seem less important. The coveted goals of former years lose their fascination and charm. He has grown in wisdom. In retrospect, he realizes his former folly and is tempted to wallow in vain regret. In this frame of mind, not realizing that life is made primarily for learning agape love, not for worldly success, one could wish that he might go back and live his life over again, using the wisdom that life has bestowed upon him. He may feel that, for him, life has been a monumental failure. But from God's standpoint, if one has learned love, there would be no point in living life over again, because the real purpose of life has been achieved. "For life, with all it yields of joy or woe and hope and fear is just our chance o' the prize of learning love" (Browning).

Life Without Love Is Disaster

The person who has made the most spectacular success, but who reaches life's end without learning love, has actually failed.

Do not envy those in the limelight of publicity, those with scintillating intellects, or those who have accumulated great wealth and all that it affords. If one has not learned love in the process, his life is a virtual disaster. Read Psalm 37. It is very relevant here.

Life is for learning love, not for sensual pleasure or for accumulating riches or fame; not for building great manufacturing, commercial, or military empires or political power. It is not for exploration, travel or conquest of outer space. It is not for learning science, history, economics, philosophy or even theology; not for delivering great orations, preaching great sermons or holding immense religious campaigns, not for the building of great institutions, such as hospitals, churches, schools, and colleges; not for publishing books, magazines or other periodicals. All of these are of value only as they grow out of or contribute to the learning or expression of God's love.

— *The Success of Learning Love*

When one has learned love, he has succeeded in life no matter how he has failed otherwise. If all the failures in learning love in the past have at last produced this brokenness of spirit, that life has not been a failure in God's sight, because it was for this He was working. This is what God was after from the beginning, because agape love is essential for rulership in God's eternity. Indeed, love is the necessary ingredient for a truly successful life on earth—but its ultimate value is in qualifying one for eternal rulership in an economy where love is the supreme law.

The wreckage caused by the sorrow and grief intrinsic to an unloving life is the price God is willing to pay to achieve brokenness, compassion, and tenderness of spirit. All sin is against love. Success at the cost of love is failure. Winning at the cost of love is losing. *Love never fails.* When the sun has grown old, and the stars have grown cold; when the oceans and rivers have run dry; when hoary time has passed away, when the solemn footsteps of eternity echo no more, love will still endure, all measureless and strong. It is the supreme law of the universe.

— *Ode to Agape Love*

(with apologies to the apostle Paul)
Though I become as rich as Croesus, King Midas, the Rockefellers, Howard Hughes, and Paul Getty combined, and have not LOVE, I am nothing.

Though I become as powerful as Nebuchadnezzar, Alexander the Great, Charlemagne, and Napoleon all together, and have not LOVE, I am nothing.

Though I have the eloquence of Demosthenes, Cicero, Shakespeare, Daniel Webster, and Churchill, so that I can sway multitudes, and have not LOVE, I am nothing.

Though I possess the beauty and charm of Helen of Troy, Cleopatra, and Miss Universe, and have not LOVE, I am nothing.

Agape love never fails!
Though there be wealth, it shall rust and decay.
Though there be fame, it shall sink into oblivion.
Though there be political power and supremacy,
it shall burst like a bubble.
Though there be military might, it shall crumble.
Though there be tongues of eloquence, they shall be stilled.
Though there be beauty of face and form, it shall fade.
But love is forever.

When hoary time shall be no more,
When earthly thrones and kingdoms fall,

When the Ancient of Days is set upon His Judgment Seat,
When angel harps are stilled and heaven's silence
fills the universe,
Love will still be young.

When the last plane has made its flight,
The last satellite circled the globe,
The last rocket has been launched;
When the debris of the melting cosmos
has been swept afar
by the fiery tempest of God's wrath;
When the new heaven and earth leap from
the matrix of the ages—
Love will still be in its infancy.
It will never grow old, never fade, never decay.
It is life's superlative goal.
It is divine.

Therefore, make love your aim!

—Anonymous

Life is for learning agape love.

LEARNING AGAPE LOVE THROUGH AGING

Aging Is a Part of God's Design

Previously we stated that all that befalls the obedient child of God is related to the development of his character. Take, for instance, the process of aging. The world at large considers this as something to be evaded, avoided, and postponed as long as possible. All kinds of devices are employed to prolong the illusion of youth. Usually it is considered that aging is simply the natural consequence of the inexorable passing of time, to be greeted with nothing but regret. The youth cult would encourage the elderly to "think young," as though dreaming could delay the inevitable flight of time. But aging is more than an unavoidable biological process. It has a purpose, and it is a part of God's design.

A Revision of Values

One of God's purposes in the process of aging is to enable us to properly revise our system of values. How different are the priorities of youth and age. In youth one's goal is success, power, fame, rank, reputation, skill, wealth, and ease. Youth often believes that life is made primarily for pleasure. *Self* is the center. God intends that the vicissitudes of life, its disappointments, heartbreaks, and the infirmities of advancing years, will change this. It is meant to disenchant one with earth and orient him heavenward. J. R. Miller says, "True living is really a succession of battles in which the better triumphs over the worse, the spirit over the flesh. Until we cease to live for self, we have not begun to live at all."'

"My Master"

An unknown author has eloquently and vividly described the transition from youth's vain ambitions to selfless devotion to the Master in the following stanzas:

I had walked life's path with an easy tread,
 Had followed where comforts and pleasures led,
Until one day, in a quiet place,
 I met my Master, face to face.

With station and rank and wealth for my goal,
 Much thought for my body—but none for my soul,
I had entered to win in life's mad race,
 When I met my Master, face to face.

I had built my castles and reared them high,
 Till their towers pierced the blue of the sky;
I had sworn to rule with an iron mace—
 When I met my Master, face to face.

I met Him, and knew Him, and blushed to see
 That His eyes full of sorrow were fixed on me;

And I faltered, and fell at His feet that day,
While my castles melted and vanished away.

Melted and vanished, and in their place
Naught else did I see but my Master's face;
And I cried aloud, "O make me meet
To follow the steps of Thy wounded feet!"

My thought is now for the souls of men;
I have lost my life to find it again,
E'er since that day, in a quiet place,
I met my Master, face to face.

The Purpose of the Passing Years

The purpose of the passing years, with their joys and sorrows, is to wean one from self-worship—to mature him in love. Getting older is not getting better unless it delivers us from self-love. Growing older is intended to make one more gentle, more thoughtful and considerate, more gracious and sympathetic, less childish and demanding. This is the reason for the trials and tribulations, the conflicts with pain, the struggles with disease, the financial reverses, the ingratitude of loved ones, the disappointments of false friendships, wrongful suffering, and the grief of bereavement.

— *Aging Is God's Finishing School*

J. R. Miller says, "Fruits are developed and ripened by the influence of weather and the climate. It takes all the different seasons, with their variety of climatic conditions, to bring fruit to maturity. Winter does its part as well as spring, summer, and autumn. Night and day, cloud and sunshine, cold and heat, wind and calm, all work together to ripen the fruit."[2]

In like manner, all life's varied experiences, even down to old age, are working together to mature and ripen *character* and develop agape love in us. All sunshine would not make good fruit, nor would all gladness and joy produce the richest character. Darkness as well as light; rough, cold weather as well as gentle, warm summer are needed to mature and enrich character in agape love.

Aging, therefore, is not something to be endured as an unfortunate but unavoidable evil. It is a part of God's plan. When properly accepted, it may constitute God's finishing school for character education and enrichment before entering eternity.

Wasting Retirement Years

Gerontologists are concerned that early retirement is an unnecessary waste of manpower. Nowhere is this truer than in the life of the aging believer. The great temptation following retirement is to follow the pattern of the world and simply do one's own pleasure. Upon retirement, those sufficiently affluent often decide that now is the time to satisfy their own desires and do the things they had always wanted to do. They often embark upon a program of travel, sightseeing, entertainment, and other forms of self-pleasing. Others, less affluent, may spend their time in frustration, bemoaning their fate, envying others, and languishing in self-pity. Believers indulging in these vices are *wasting their sorrows.*

— *Making Retirement Productive*

God desires to utilize for the specific purpose of intercession the long period of physical decline that comes to many people.

Spiritually, this can be the most productive period of life. In *Destined for the Throne*, it is shown that "prayer is where the action is," that "the most important thing anyone can do for God or man is to pray"; that "you can do more than pray *after* you have prayed, but you cannot do more than pray *until* you have prayed"; that "the church, through believing prayer, holds the balance of power both in world affairs and in the salvation of individual souls"; and that "the fate of the world is in the hands of nameless saints."

Satanic Strategy

Since this is true, elderly and retired people could and should be the greatest force available to God in influencing world affairs and the salvation of souls. During active life it is more difficult to find sufficient time to pray. Pastors, evangelists, administrators, and other Christian workers are in the same dilemma. Unless they have been well taught concerning the importance of prayer and the devotional life, they are in grave danger of relegating it to a place of secondary importance. Satan's most successful strategy is to keep Christian workers so busy in secondary things that they have little time for the primary thing— *prayer*. Thus the "good" becomes the enemy of the "best."

All of the most heinous forms of evil in the world are the result of demon activity. The only power that controls them is the power of the Holy Spirit. And the Holy Spirit, by His own choice, is released to do His work only by the prayers of holy people (Matthew 16:18–19; John 20:21–23).[3] This is why John Wesley said, "God will do nothing but in answer to prayer."

Priority of Prayer

From heaven's standpoint, all spiritual victories are won not primarily in the pulpit, not primarily in the bright lights of publicity, nor yet through the ostentatious blaring of trumpets, but in the secret place of prayer. . . . Thank God for the gifts, talents, and preaching ability of men like Billy Graham. This is not an effort to depreciate these assets. But the power that has transformed multiplied thousands through Billy Graham's ministry is not the power of superior gifts, unusual talents, brilliant rhetoric, or psychological persuasiveness, but the power released by the prayer and faith of millions of his prayer helpers. From heaven's standpoint, the combined prayer and intercession that surrounds and supports Billy Graham is the real explanation of what is taking place. Because of the immense program of prayer warfare on his behalf, Satan's legions opposing his efforts are overcome and bound in the same way they were when Moses, Aaron, and Hur interceded for Joshua and Israel against Amalek.[4]

Prayer Is Where the Action Is

Many people grieve because they have been denied service on the mission field or in some other chosen endeavor. Through faithful intercession they may accomplish as much and reap as full a reward as though they had been on the field in person. Those who lament that they have been cheated in life because they have no shining gifts or spectacular talents, or those who have been retired by age or illness, may, through faithful intercession, share in the heavenly reward equally with the most highly endowed, all because prayer is where the action is. "Anyone who receives a prophet because he is a prophet will receive a prophet's reward, and anyone who receives a righteous man because he is a righteous man will receive a righteous man's reward" (Matthew 10:41). If simple hospitality brings equal compensation, then a prayer support ministry will surely not go unrewarded.[5]

— *Prayer Warfare Is Running Interference*

There is only one Billy Graham. There will never be another. But according to the principle articulated by Jesus in the above-quoted Scripture, the lowliest saint who faithfully labors in prayer on Graham's behalf will as surely share in his reward as if he personally possessed all the gifts with which God has endowed the famous evangelist.

This same principle applies in the work of any and every spiritual leader. To the extent that one is faithful in prayer warfare on behalf of those God has placed in positions of responsibility and leadership in soul-winning and kingdom affairs, such as missionaries, pastors, evangelists, teachers, administrators—to that extent he will share in the eternal reward that will be meted out to these workers in that day. To use an athletic metaphor: Prayer warfare is running interference for the one who is carrying the ball.

The Fate of the World

This leaves no room for self-pity or envy of those more gifted, provided one is willing to fill his place as a prayer warrior. In heaven's "book" the nameless saint in the most remote and secluded spot, completely lost to view, and overshadowed in the battle, is just as important, and if he is faithful, will receive just as great a reward as the most heralded and gifted leader. Hallelujah! All of the faithful prayer warriors are just as truly at the front and are making just as great a contribution in the fray as the apparent leader. And they will share equally in the reward. Verily, "The fate of the world is in the hands of nameless saints."[6]

— *A Viable Alternative*

If these things are true, then no believer needs ever to retire and no period of life needs to be unproductive. By means of intercession, he can be as truly in the front line in a wheelchair or an invalid's bed as those who are active on their feet. It requires and develops more character to pray than to preach, sing, or organize city-wide campaigns. There are enough elderly believers (many of whom feel they are laid on the shelf and useless) who, if they could see that prayer is the most important thing anyone can do for God or man, and would be willing to discipline themselves to a life of prayer—there are enough of them to turn this nation around; and praying saints are the only ones who can! "The righteous will flourish like a palm tree. . . . They will still bear fruit in old age" (Psalm 92:12, 14). It is sad that any elderly believer should waste what could be his most productive years in self-pleasing or self-pity.

The following lines suggest a viable alternative:

> *I cannot go on—I wonder why!*
> *Is my life spent, will I soon die?*
> *If I could have another life to live—*
> *But no! He only gives us one in which*
> *To gain or lose a crown.*
>
> *O come, my soul! Thou still dost live;*
> *Why languish longer? Arise and give*
> *Thy best to the task. The night comes on.*
> *Thou art not too old—who said you were?*
> *God sets no age—not in His Word,*
> *Though Satan in his subtle way*
> *Has set you back, no longer stay.*

Arise! And give what you have left
  To make Christ known to souls bereft.
His hand leads on, pray follow fast,
  The time grows short, then heav'n at last.[7]
                    —*Alvin A. Rasmussen*

Remember, you are destined for the throne! God is training you now. Your trials are not an accident: No suffering is purposeless. Your eternal profit is in view. Therefore, *don't waste your sorrows!*

Endnotes

A Word From the Author

1. Agape love is the love that loves because of its own inherent nature, not because of the excellence or worth of its object. According to the Bible dictionary, it is spontaneous, automatic love.

Introduction

1. From Amy Carmichael, *Gold Cord* (Fort Washington, PA: Christian Literature Crusade, 1974, and London: SPCK, 1932). Used by permission.

Chapter 2

1. According to the *New Testament and Wycliffe Bible Commentary,* the term *adoption* in certain Bible passages is not used in the modern sense. Rather, it refers to one being placed in the position of a grown son. It is the formal and ceremonial recognition of a born son as having reached adulthood.

CHAPTER 3

1. Paul E. Billheimer, *Destined for the Throne* (Minneapolis: Bethany House, 1975), revised, 1996, chapter 6.

CHAPTER 5

1. Alexander Maclaren, *Exposition of Hebrews*, 234.
2. *The New Testament and Wycliffe Bible Commentary* (Chicago: Moody Press, 1971; New York: The Iversen-Norman Associates), 909.
3. Oswald Chambers, *My Utmost for His Highest* (New York: Dodd, Mead & Company, 1935), 252. Used by permission.
4. Sheridan Baker, *Hidden Manna* (Chicago and Boston: The Christian Witness Co., 1903), 51, 53.
5. Used by permission of Evangelical Publishers, a division of Scripture Press Publications, Ltd., Whitby, Ontario.

CHAPTER 6

1. "To resume my history, the smallpox had so much hurt one of my eyes, that it was feared I would lose it. The gland at the corner of my eye was injured. An imposthume arose from time to time between the nose and the eye, which gave me great pain till it was lanced. It swelled all my head to the degree that I could not bear even a pillow. The least noise was agony to me, though sometimes they made a great commotion in my chamber. Yet this was a precious time to me, for two reasons. First, because I was left in bed alone, where I had a sweet retreat without interruption; the other, because it answered the desire I had for suffering— which desire was so great, that all the austerities of the body would have been but as a drop of water to quench so great a fire. Indeed the severities and rigors which I then exercised were extreme, but they did not appease this appe-

tite for the cross. It is Thou alone, O Crucified Saviour, who canst make the cross truly effectual for the death of self. Let others bless themselves in their ease or gaity, grandeur or pleasures, poor temporary heavens; for me, my desires were all turned another way, even to the silent path of suffering for Christ, and to be united to Him, through the mortification of all that was of nature in me, that my senses, appetites and will, being dead to these, might wholly live in Him."—Madame Guyon, *Madame Guyon* [autobiography] (Chicago: Moody Press), 140–41.

CHAPTER 7

1. Billheimer, chapter 1.
2. Ibid., chapter 2.
3. No physical relationship is implied.
4. Billheimer, 35.

CHAPTER 8

1. J. R. Miller, *When the Song Begins*, 39.
2. A. N. Hodgkin, *Christ in All the Scriptures* (Glasgow: Pickering & Inglis, 1908), 86–87.

CHAPTER 9

1. C. S. Lovett, *Unequally Yoked Wives* (Baldwin Park, CA: Personal Christianity, 1968). Used by permission.
2. J. R. Miller, *Weekday Religion*, 67–68.
3. O. Hobart Mowrer, *The Crisis in Psychiatry and Religion* (Princeton: D. Van Nostrand Company, Inc., 1961).
4. O. Hobart Mowrer, ed., *Amorality and Mental Health* (Chicago: Rand McNally & Company, 1967), 56.
5. Ibid., 17.
6. Ibid., 301.

CHAPTER 10

1. J. R. Miller, *Upper Currents*, "God's Slow Making of Us."

CHAPTER 11

1. J. R. Miller, *The Ministry of Comfort* (London, Hodder & Stoughton, 1901), 30.
2. Chambers, 306. Used by permission.
3. Billheimer, "Ecclesiastical Treadmills," 101.

CHAPTER 12

1. J. R. Miller, *Making the Most of Life*, 2.
2. Miller, *Upper Currents*, 94.
3. Billheimer, 43–51.
4. Ibid., 104–105.
5. Ibid., 105–106.
6. Ibid., 106.
7. Alvin A. Rasmussen, "You're Not Too Old." First published in *Brown Gold*, magazine of the New Tribes Mission, Woodworth, WI. Adapted. Used by permission of the author.